Every once in a while ...
truth from the Scriptur...
context that literally alt...
Your Light is that kind...

JENTEZEN FRANKLIN
SENIOR PASTOR, FREE CHAPEL
NEW YORK TIMES BEST-SELLING AUTHOR

Pastor Joakim is an authentic and brilliant story-teller who brings God's Word to life through inspiring stories and applicable truths. *Shine Your Light* is encouraging, engaging, and equipping for our generation as we grab hold of the truth of our unique call in God. I am grateful for this incredible gift that leaves us motivated to go and be the light of the world!

ELAINE FISHER
PASTOR, GATEWAY CHURCH HOUSTON

In *Shine Your Light*, Joakim Lundqvist eloquently captures the essence of what it means to live out the biblical truth that "God is light; in him there is no darkness at all" (1 John 1:5). This book transcends simple spiritual guidance, offering actionable steps for anyone eager to embrace their role as a beacon in the darkness. Joakim's approach is as practical as it is inspirational, reflecting his own joyful spirit in every chapter. As a close friend, I have always admired how his presence subtly uplifts those around him, a quality that resonates through his written words. *Shine Your Light* is essential reading for anyone ready to discover and use their unique gifts to spread God's love. I wholeheartedly endorse this transformative work, confident it will inspire readers to make a real difference in their communities.

—PASTOR JONATHAN STOCKSTILL
BETHANY CHURCH, BATON ROUGE

Shine Your
Light

Shine Your Light

JOAKIM LUNDQVIST

 CHARISMA HOUSE

SHINE YOUR LIGHT by Joakim Lundqvist
Published by Charisma House, an imprint of Charisma Media
1150 Greenwood Blvd., Lake Mary, Florida 32746

For more resources like this, visit MyCharismaShop.com and the author's website at pastorjoakim.com.

Cataloging-in-Publication Data is on file with the Library of Congress.
International Standard Book Number: 978-1-63641-397-6
E-book ISBN: 978-1-63641-398-3

1 2024

Printed in the United States of America

Most Charisma Media products are available at special quantity discounts for bulk purchase for sales promotions, premiums, fund-raising, and educational needs. For details, call us at (407) 333-0600 or visit our website at www.charismamedia.com.

To Maria

This is the message we have heard from him and declare to you: God is light; in him there is no darkness at all.

—1 JOHN 1:5

CONTENTS

Contents

FOREWORD

*I*F YOU COULD sit down for coffee with Joakim Lundqvist, you would quickly discover that he's the real deal. His life has clearly been transformed by the love of Jesus, and it doesn't take long to feel that love radiating from him. Joakim's authenticity and sincerity are evident in every conversation, every sermon, and every encounter.

God has used Joakim's genuine faith to change lives around the world. He is senior pastor of the largest church in Sweden, but his influence extends far beyond the borders of his homeland. Now based in the United States, he travels extensively, sharing the message of Christ with a world often shrouded in darkness. His mission is clear: to be a bright light shining in a dark world and to inspire others to do the same.

Sharing his faith is as natural as breathing for Joakim. He embodies the Great Commission with a grace and ease that is both inspiring and accessible. Yet he understands that for many of us, sharing our faith can be daunting. Fear, hesitation, and a lack of confidence often hold us back from fully embracing our calling to be witnesses for Christ.

In his new book, *Shine Your Light*, Joakim offers a down-to-earth approach to sharing your faith in Jesus. Deeply rooted in Scripture, this book isn't a collection of abstract principles or lofty ideals. It's a practical guide filled with insights to help you grow in your faith and share it with others, no matter where you are on your spiritual journey.

So if you want to make a difference in the lives of others but feel inadequate, I encourage you to take Joakim's words to heart as he motivates you to step out of your comfort zone and into what God is calling you to do. I pray that this book will empower you to overcome your fears, build your confidence, and embrace your role as a daily witness for Christ as we work together to grow the kingdom.

In a time when darkness seems to prevail, this timely and powerful message will remind you that we're all called to be the light of the world. Let this must-read book be your guide as you embark on the path to shining your light for Christ.

—CRAIG GROESCHEL
PASTOR OF LIFE.CHURCH AND
NEW YORK TIMES BEST-SELLING AUTHOR

PART I

LET THERE BE *Light*!

This is the message we have heard from him and declare to you: God is light; in him there is no darkness at all.

—1 JOHN 1:5

Chapter 1

LIGHT—THE NATURE OF GOD

*H*ow I WISH I had heard and understood the simple message of 1 John 1:5 long before I actually did.

Even though I was born and raised in Sweden, the second most secular country in the world, I thought I knew the basics about Christianity due to my father being a priest in the Lutheran state church. And he was far from the only priest in the family. Both my grandfathers and four of my uncles also shared this profession, so from the outside one could easily think that little Joakim was heading straight for heaven.

However, through the years the Lutheran state church of Sweden has tragically devolved into more of a cultural institution than a genuine church founded on the Word of God. My parents did their best to take me to church on Sundays and teach me the basics of Christianity, but not being secure in their own faith themselves, what was passed on to me was a fragile construction of religious thoughts and beliefs that made little sense.

I was taught that God was almighty, which I assumed meant that whatever happened in the world reflected His perfect will. I mean, if He wanted things to be different and had all power, He would have just changed them, right? Then again, when I looked at what was going on in the world—wars, famine, violence, oppression, diseases—I concluded that I didn't really want to be around this God very much. If He had all power and this was His preferred outcome, then sorry, I prefer to be anywhere but close to Him.

You could say that growing up my relationship to God was

3

pretty much like that of a child with a parent who is an alcoholic. It was all about trying to stay close enough to make sure I was allowed to go to heaven when I died while constantly keeping a safe distance since I had no way of knowing if God wanted to hug me or hit me today.

Thinking of my teenage years, I am reminded of words from the Book of Hosea: "My people are destroyed from lack of knowledge" (Hos. 4:6). Because I lacked knowledge about the true nature and character of God, I developed a religious idea that was actually closer to Islam than Christianity. One of the most-used phrases by Muslims is "Inshallah," which is Arabic for "If God wants"—a phrase Muslims add to almost every sentence that deals with future. "See you tomorrow, inshallah," "Let's meet up next week, inshallah," "I'll go shopping tomorrow, inshallah." Since God is completely unpredictable, and you can never tell what He wants or what He will do, good or bad, you'd better be prepared for anything. This was the reality of my faith at the time, so not really the ideal foundation for a healthy relationship with God.

At age fourteen I started to slip away from it all, secretly at first since I didn't have the guts to tell my parents I wanted nothing to do with their God. Still attending mass, I disconnected inside and was more and more annoyed with religion as a whole. Then at fifteen I cut whatever was left of the umbilical cord attaching me to cathedrals with stained-glass windows and that seemingly schizophrenic God who lived inside them. I turned my back on every aspect of my Christian background by trying to become the worst sinner I could be: drinking, partying, doing drugs. Still, my heart was aching, as I knew deep inside that this was all a charade, a part I tried to play in a world I didn't belong to.

Looking back now, I realize I was in a Jonah situation. I was on my boat heading for Tarshish, trying to get as far away from the ways of the Lord as possible. I had the calling of God on my life, which made me a pathetic sinner even though I tried my best to be the perfect one. But you can never outrun God.

BAMBOOZLED BY A BUDDY

One day when I was sixteen, a drinking buddy got in touch. He said a great New Years' Eve party was coming up in Uppsala, a city about three hours' drive away. He went on and on about how there would be booze and pretty girls and what a great time we would have. Would I come along? Sure, why not. Sounded like fun.

We decided to go there together and spend the New Year partying. Little did I know that the "party" he invited me to was in fact a youth revival conference. My friend was a lost grandchild of God just like me, with Christian parents but without a personal encounter with Jesus, now running away from God. In the weeks leading up to giving me this invitation, he had heard about this youth revival, listened to some cassette tapes with powerful Christian messages, and considered giving God a second chance in his life. As my friend, and realizing I too was trying to run away from God, he basically lied to me in Jesus' name to get me to come along with him.

When we finally arrived at the "party" building, instead of finding a dance floor, drugs, and alcohol, we entered a room with about a hundred teenagers singing songs of worship to Jesus. I had never seen anything like it in my life. The only church music I had ever been exposed to were ancient hymns with strange words accompanied by a thundering organ. Hearing these young people my own age singing so passionately and lifting their hands—something I had never seen either—caught me completely off guard. My first instinct, to punch my friend in the face for lying to me, slowly faded, and

5

I just stood there frozen at the back of the room. Listening. Watching. Experiencing a presence I had felt before during a few holy moments of my childhood.

God was here.

Still, I struggled. Looking at the young people in the room worshipping, part of me wanted to somehow join in, but another part said a very distinct no. My problem was not that I didn't believe God existed. It was that I didn't trust Him. How could I, when He was obviously both good and evil, loving and tyrannical at the same time.

The worship came to an end, and a guy in his twenties stepped up, opened his Bible, and read from 1 John 1:5: "God is light; in him there is no darkness at all."

The verse hit me like a ton of bricks. I had never heard it in my life. Was this the Bible? Did he just say that God was only light and no darkness?

He went on to talk about how God is always true to His character, that He is only light, only love, only holiness, and that His will for us is only good. We, as human beings, have our own free will and can exercise it to do good or evil, and the world is a sad reflection of our failures and unwillingness to do what is right. But God is only light. This is why we can trust Him. This is why we can place our lives in His hands.

As I listened, I felt God performing a heart surgery of love inside me. For the very first time I began to understand that the God who was calling my name was a God of light only. A God that could be trusted. A God I could get to know personally. Tears poured down my face as it all finally made sense. I was like the prodigal coming home. So what was I supposed to do now? How was I supposed to respond to this?

The guy up front said, "If you are here tonight, and you don't have a relationship with God, you can come to the front..." He didn't have to say anything more. I was already up there with him. Joined by my friend and about ten other young people, I prayed my first honest prayer to God: "Forgive me. Receive me. Save me. Use me."

As I prayed while crying like a baby, I had no idea that this would be the turning point of my whole life. That it would be the step that launched me into an adventure of a lifetime together with Jesus. And that I would go on to serve Him full-time, pastor the largest church in Sweden, see a youth movement of tens of thousands of teenagers rise up, and preach the gospel of Jesus in over sixty nations.

This turning point did not primarily consist of a radical experience or an emotional high. Instead it came about through a Bible verse the Holy Spirit opened my eyes to—one that taught me that God is light. All light. Only light. All love. Only love. All good. Only good. And that because He is, He can be trusted.

Why Christianity Stands Out

This is one of the things that makes Christianity stand out from all other religions. Almost every religious ideology involves a deity to be worshipped. But that godhead is rarely described in detail. Yet why should it be, if the role of humans is simply to submit, honor, and worship? A slave has no business knowing his master personally. But here is where the story of the gospel is completely different. It is one about a God who has created you not just to obey and serve Him but to have an intimate, personal relationship with Him.

The most well-known Bible verse in the world tells us that "God so loved the world that he gave his one and only Son, that whoever believes in him shall not perish but have eternal life" (John 3:16). It stresses that the whole point of the Father sending Jesus and Him dying for us was to provide us with *eternal life.* So how do we define this eternal life? It cannot only be about eternal existence since the Bible clearly teaches that every human being will exist forever somewhere, regardless of whether they believe in Christ or not.

The true definition of eternal life is given to us by Jesus Himself as He prays His very last prayer for His disciples before being crucified the next day:

> Now this is eternal life: that they know you, the only
> true God, and Jesus Christ, whom you have sent.
> —JOHN 17:3

Eternal life is not just an eternity in heaven. Eternal life is to know God, starting here and now!

Jesus did not sacrifice His life just to give you a ticket to glory when you die. He did it so that you could know God personally and walk in a daily, beautiful, unbroken personal relationship with your Father. He did it to restore the intimacy that was broken through the fall of man.

Intimacy always requires security, stability, and trust. This is exactly why God is so concerned that you know that you know that you know: He is light. Only light. Nothing but light. If there is darkness in your life, God is not its author. He doesn't use darkness to punish you or to teach you anything since darkness is the opposite of His nature and He will not deny Himself by using it as a tool.

New Age and Eastern religions have tried to hijack the word *light* and often use terms such as *enlightenment* or *enlightened.* That doesn't really make sense at all for one simple reason: light always brings clarity. Light makes us see things we couldn't see before. When the light is turned on, we see clearly. Yet these religions that use "light" high and low are among the vaguest in the world, all based on feelings, emotions, experiences, and energies, with no clear vision or image of God at all. How contradictory to speak so much about light and still have no clarity.

Yet our God is the true light—a light that reveals and enables us to see and know His nature, His goodness and love, and allows us the knowledge and assurance we need to trust Him, surrender to Him completely, and live our lives for His glory.

> For you were once darkness, but now you are light in the Lord. Live as children of light (for the fruit of the light consists in all goodness, righteousness and truth) and find out what pleases the Lord.
>
> —EPHESIANS 5:8–10

Your first step of the journey to "live as children of light" is just that: trust in Him. He is worthy to be trusted. For He is light, and in Him there is no darkness at all.

Chapter 2

LET THERE BE LIGHT!

I WANT YOU TO notice that 1 John 1:5, the verse that has been our main focus so far, does not teach us that God has light, that He is the creator of light, or that light is part of His being.

It says God *is* light.

Let's look at it again:

> This is the message we have heard from him and
> declare to you: God is light; in him there is no dark-
> ness at all.
>
> —1 JOHN 1:5

This means light is not one of His characteristics, tools, or assets. Instead, the Bible says light is His essence, His nature, His whole being.

Therefore, everything about our God is about light and all the things that light represents: purity, clarity, holiness, love, goodness, truth, and revelation.

Wherever God goes, light will follow.

Whatever God does, light will be released.

Wherever God is, light will be all around.

And whatever God touches and claims ownership of will be illuminated by His light. We see this principle expressed throughout the entire Scripture.

> When Moses came down from Mount Sinai with the
> two tablets of the covenant law in his hands, he was
> not aware that his face was radiant because he had
> spoken with the LORD. When Aaron and all the

Israelites saw Moses, his face was radiant, and they were afraid to come near him.

When Moses finished speaking to them, he put a veil over his face. But whenever he entered the LORD's presence to speak with him, he removed the veil until he came out. And when he came out and told the Israelites what he had been commanded, they saw that his face was radiant. Then Moses would put the veil back over his face until he went in to speak with the LORD.

—EXODUS 34:29–30, 33–35

Remember, this is way before Christ, the perfect Lamb of God, had been slain for the sins of the world, giving us full access to God's presence through the blood of Jesus. Sin still separated God from fully communicating with even His own covenant people. When Moses requested to see God's glory (Exod. 33:18), his wish was only partially granted. He would see God, but only His back, since the Lord told him, "You cannot see my face, for no one may see me and live" (Exod. 33:20).

God then passed him by, and Moses saw just this little glimpse of God and His glory. Yet when he came back down to the camp, his face was shining so much that the people of Israel were afraid to approach him.

Even that glimpse of God was enough for the essence and nature of God—light—to rub off on and completely illuminate His servant Moses to the point that his face shone with bright light.

And of course if this was already the case in the Old Testament, how much more should not the light of God be expressed on and through us, who have the incredible privilege to live on the other side of Calvary, the other side of the veil torn in the temple, the other side of the empty grave? As Paul says:

> And we all, who with unveiled faces contemplate the Lord's glory, are being transformed into his image with ever-increasing glory.
>
> —2 Corinthians 3:18

Another beautiful example of the light of God demonstrated in the Old Testament is found in how the priests were commanded to bless the people of Israel. This is the origin of what is called the priestly blessing (*Birkat Kohanim*), in Judaism sometimes referred to as the "raising of the hands":

> The Lord said to Moses, "Tell Aaron and his sons, 'This is how you are to bless the Israelites. Say to them: "The Lord bless you and keep you; the Lord make his face shine on you and be gracious to you; the Lord turn his face toward you and give you peace."'"
>
> —Numbers 6:22–26

Again we see light, the essence and nature of God, being so central in the spoken blessing over Israel. Note that the blessing itself is quite short and nowhere near an endless list of promises concerning every area of human life. But Israel knew that the light of God shining on them represented His fullness, His goodness, His love, His holiness, and His perfection. As long as His light was upon them, they knew they would have all they could possibly need!

In the last few verses of the Bible, we also see a glimpse of God's light displayed in what is about to come: the New Jerusalem. In the few verses available to us in Revelation, this new city of God that comes down from heaven at the end of all things is not described in great detail. We are allowed some facts about its overall size, its walls, and the material of its doors. However, the one thing we are told apart from the technical information is the most important thing of all: the city is radiant, fully illuminated by the light of God!

> And he carried me away in the Spirit to a mountain great and high, and showed me the Holy City, Jerusalem, coming down out of heaven from God. It shone with the glory of God, and its brilliance was like that of a very precious jewel, like a jasper, clear as crystal.
>
> —REVELATION 21:10–11

> The city does not need the sun or the moon to shine on it, for the glory of God gives it light, and the Lamb is its lamp. The nations will walk by its light, and the kings of the earth will bring their splendor into it. On no day will its gates ever be shut, for there will be no night there.
>
> —REVELATION 21:23–25

How amazing!

The New Jerusalem is shining to the point where no sun or moon is needed anymore. God Himself is its source of light. The Lamb is its lamp, and the nations will walk in this glorious, pure light that is the essence and nature of God Himself.

Having read about the light of God in these final verses of the Bible, let us rewind to the very first ones. Now brace yourselves because we are about to journey into a revelation that may well change your life if you get ahold of it. And it starts in the opening words of the Bible, in Genesis chapter 1, the story of creation:

> In the beginning God created the heavens and the earth. Now the earth was formless and empty, darkness was over the surface of the deep, and the Spirit of God was hovering over the waters. And God said, "Let there be light," and there was light.
>
> —GENESIS 1:1–3

The God who is light has now found it in His heart to launch a creation. In the days to follow, creativity will be released like never before or after. The great Artist is about to create the masterpiece of eternity, reflecting the many facets of His being, and pour the beauty and diversity of His essence into such a spectacular creation that we still to this day have not seen the full extent of it.

But before launching this explosion of creativity, resulting in millions of species—animals, fishes, birds, plants, trees, and finally His own image, man—before any of these are spoken into being, He says: "Let there be light." First, let there be light. Before anything else, let there be light.

The first words ever spoken by God and recorded in the Bible were a commandment for light to appear—a proclamation into existence of the very essence of His own being and nature. Whatever is about to be created from chaos, whatever will be called into existence from nothingness, will be birthed into the light of God, into the presence of Him who is Himself light.

First the light is turned on. Then God's creative power is released.

First the light is turned on. Then miracles can happen.

First the light is turned on. Then nothing is impossible.

First the light is turned on. Then God starts to work.

My friend, God is the same yesterday, today, and forever (Heb. 13:8). He has not changed. He still operates by the same principles. If He started His work in the dawn of creation by first turning on the light, then got to work creating and changing, He will do so again today in your life and through your life. We will keep coming back to this divine principle throughout the rest of this book, and I will keep explaining to you, step by step and in detail, the incredible power found in this statement.

But before we move on in that direction, let me share an amazing testimony with you.

A CHURCH OF FEAR OR A CHURCH OF FAITH?

Back in 2016 and 2017 my continent, Europe, suddenly found itself faced with a humanitarian disaster. Tens of thousands of refugees from the Middle East were fleeing the terror of ISIS. Trying to escape death, rape, and torture, many families got into simple, inflatable boats heading into the Mediterranean Sea, aiming for safety in Europe.

When all this started to happen, Europe were taken completely off guard by the events. Few could even imagine the level of desperation that would make a father and mother bring their children on board an inflatable boat and simply hope for the best out on the open ocean. Our newspapers filled up with pictures of drowned children whose bodies had been washed up along the shores of Turkey and Greece, and we realized we were facing a genuine humanitarian emergency—something the scale of which we had not experienced in decades. We also quickly understood what would happen if and when the boats with these families made it to Athens, Greece, in the southern tip of Europe. They would start walking north, heading for Germany or my nation, Sweden, which at the time had very liberal immigration laws. For reference, walking by foot from

Athens to Sweden is equal to walking from Dallas, Texas, to Miami, Florida.

Facing this scenario, Sweden panicked. We are a small nation and realized we would hardly be able to handle refugee immigration on this scale. Media was raging, politicians were all over the place, and even Christian leaders spoke out in fear, claiming "the Muslims are coming to take over!" At this time, I took my core team of pastors aside for prayer, asking God what to do and how to position ourselves in this brand-new scenario. And I will never forget the words He spoke to my heart at that moment: "Joakim, do you want to build a church of fear or a church of faith?" I replied, "Lord, I want to build a church of faith!" Again I was reminded: faith does not deny the problem but chooses to focus on the potential inside the problem. Faith does not deny the obstacle but chooses to focus on the opportunity inside the obstacle.

Now, I was not a supporter of the liberal immigration laws of Sweden at the time, and I fully understood that by accepting all these refugees, we would import truckloads of social problems into our nation. There was no question about that, and time has proved it to be true. However, these displaced people were coming regardless. There was nothing we could do about it, leaving us with two choices: we could distance ourselves from the whole situation and complain about it on Facebook, or we could step into the fray in Jesus' name and dare to believe that somewhere inside this humanitarian disaster there would be a seed of revival.

Among the first steps we took to minister God's love and the gospel of Jesus was to set up a "Welcome to Europe" station on the shores of Athens to give the incoming refugees food, clothes, and medical care if needed, and then direct them on how to proceed north. Every week we flew teams of young people from our church in Sweden, in the north of Europe, down to Greece in the south to man this station and provide first aid to the people that came off the boats.

Later in this book I will tell you more about everything that happened through our initiatives to reach out to the Muslim refugees and of the supernatural revival that became its outcome. But for now let me just share one story—one testimony out of hundreds—reminding us of what we have been studying in this chapter: that first the light is turned on, then God starts to work.

"IF YOU ARE HUNGRY..."

Among all the fleeing refugees was one family that had escaped all the way from Afghanistan. The father, mother, and six children had been living in a house outside Kabul, the capital, when one day a Taliban warrior knocked on their door. As the father opened the door, the warrior demanded that the father give up his twelve-year-old daughter to become his wife. The father desperately tried to talk him out of it, realizing what a nightmare of a life would await his daughter, but finally he was given an ultimatum: the Taliban warrior would come back with his army the next day, and the father would be left with the choice of either giving his daughter away or having the entire family killed.

That night, as the rest of the family went to sleep without knowing about the horrible threat they were facing, the father rolled out his prayer mat and faced Mecca. He called out to Allah for help, asking him to please save this precious girl and the lives of the family. But as he desperately prayed, the father slowly realized that although he had been praying to Allah all his life, no prayer had ever been answered. Why would he expect these prayers to be different?

Then suddenly the father remembered that someone once

told him there was a Christian God who was all good, all love, and heard the prayers offered to Him. So in the darkness of the night, this Muslim man started calling out: "O Christian God! O Christian God! If You are out there and can hear me, please help me! Please save my daughter!"

In one second the room was filled with a radiant, warm light that illuminated everything around the father. Though the light was completely unexpected, he wasn't afraid. There was a peace to the light and a presence in it that filled him with love and hope.

In the middle of the light, the Muslim father saw a Man standing there smiling at him. He started to speak, but He did not introduce Himself by name. Instead He said:

> When you are hungry, I will give you food. When you are naked, I will give you clothes. When you are hopeless, I will give you hope. When you are in the darkness, I will give you light.

The Man then told the father to wake his family up, pack their essentials, and flee to the south. To make a much longer story a bit shorter, the family fled Afghanistan, headed south, and ended up in one of the many inflatable boats of refugees that were headed for Europe. And as their boat finally approached Athens, at the southern tip of our continent, the first thing the Muslim father and his family saw was our "Welcome to Europe" station and the team of young people from Word of Life Church. Standing on the beach, they were holding up four large signs saying:

"If you are hungry, we have food"

"If you are naked, we have clothes"

"If you are hopeless, we have hope"

"If you are in the darkness, we have light"

These were the exact words the Man of shining light had introduced Himself by in Afghanistan weeks earlier! The Muslim father realized that these young people from our church were connected to the God of light that had appeared to him, and he and his whole family accepted Christ as their Lord.

Praise the name of Jesus forever and ever!

This story keeps bringing tears to my eyes. I love the way God heard this man's prayer from the very first second, when his old god had failed him. I love how Jesus introduced Himself to the man according to the signs He trusted we would be there to hold up at the beach in Athens weeks later.

And I love how the story of salvation began by God once again saying, "Let there be light," in the middle of this desperate father's darkest night.

First the light is turned on. Then miracles can happen.

First the light is turned on. Then nothing is impossible.

First the light is turned on. Then God starts to work.

Chapter 3

WHEN THE LIGHT WENT OUT

*D*ARKNESS.

What a horrible word and horrible state, especially for someone created and destined to live in the light of God. Darkness is not even a thing on its own; it is only the absence of something else: the absence of light.

In darkness we cannot see or move properly. In darkness our eyes are constantly searching for even the smallest little light, like remote stars in a vast, dark sky. To try to cope with darkness, since it is so unnatural to us, our pupils dilate, allowing more light to enter the eye, and the light-detecting cells in the human eye will desperately try to regenerate more rhodopsin, the protein that mediates light vision.

In Sweden, which suffers from long, dark winters with only a few hours of light per day, every baby is given additional A and D vitamins to compensate for what the light of day would normally supply. And if we've had a rainy summer with not too much sunlight, incidents of depression and even suicides increase as we again head for the dark winter.

Our whole being seems to fight this unnatural state of being without light, and the simple reason is that we are all created for light, created to be in the presence of the God who is light. In the absence of His light, we suffer—physically, mentally, spiritually.

So when did the light go out, and why? The Bible tells us the story:

> Now the serpent was more crafty than any of the
> wild animals the Lord God had made. He said to the

21

woman, "Did God really say, 'You must not eat from any tree in the garden'?" The woman said to the serpent, "We may eat fruit from the trees in the garden, but God did say, 'You must not eat fruit from the tree that is in the middle of the garden, and you must not touch it, or you will die.'"

"You will not certainly die," the serpent said to the woman. "For God knows that when you eat from it your eyes will be opened, and you will be like God, knowing good and evil."

When the woman saw that the fruit of the tree was good for food and pleasing to the eye, and also desirable for gaining wisdom, she took some and ate it. She also gave some to her husband, who was with her, and he ate it. Then the eyes of both of them were opened, and they realized they were naked; so they sewed fig leaves together and made coverings for themselves.

—GENESIS 3:1–7

This story recounts the greatest tragedy of human history: how we who were created by a God who is light and thus were designed to live in His light, rebelled against Him and sentenced ourselves to separation from Him.

Looking at the story in detail, it's clear that what gave the serpent an opportunity to tempt man was ignorance regarding what God had actually said. Eve claimed that the Lord had said, "You must not eat fruit from the tree that is in the middle of the garden, *and you must not touch it*, or you will die," which was wrong. God never said anything about not touching the fruit, only about not eating it (Gen. 2:17, emphasis added). As we allow ignorance of the Word of God into our lives, we open ourselves up to heresy, temptation, and failure. However, when we build our lives and our families on the strong foundation of the Word of God, and constantly sit under sound teaching of that Word in our local church, we stand strong.

And while we are at it, why did God have the tree of knowledge planted in the Garden of Eden at all? Why allow this opportunity for sin and separation in the first place?

The short answer to this question is because God wants His relationship with man, with you, to be based on love and not constraint. And love requires a free will.

You see, without the tree of knowledge in the garden, man would have had no choice but to stay in the presence of God. Though this would have been the best by far, love just does not work that way. You can use force to make people obey, respect, serve, and do as they're told. But no force, no lack of choice in the world, can make someone love. Love can only grow from the stem of a person's own free will.

When the devil realized that man was unsure of what God had really said or not said, he was quick to twist the words of God around to mean something different from what God initially intended.

Adam and Eve were fooled by his lies and chose to obey the prince of darkness rather than the King of light, and as a result they were expelled from the presence of God, the presence of light. This was the "death" God had talked about—one not defined by ceasing to exist but by becoming the opposite of what you were made to be. It was a "dying" in relation to man's original purpose, which was to live in fellowship with the God of light. Mankind now had to acclimatize to a whole new reality: to be created for light, yet having to live in the absence of it.

WALKING IN CIRCLES

A few years ago I came across a German scientific research project that intrigued me. These guys had chosen to study how man behaves when surrounded by complete darkness. This had nothing to do with the Christian or spiritual perspective of light, just with the natural, yet I was eager to read about the results of the study. And they were indeed fascinating!

The scientists had people enter a large open room and line up with their backs against one of its walls. Once in position, the lights were turned off, leaving the people inside the room in complete darkness, and they were instructed to try to walk in a straight line to the opposing wall.

The scientists repeated this test over and over again while detecting the movements of those aiming to cross the dark room in as straight a line as possible. And when all the data was in, the experiment came to a striking conclusion: every one of the participants, though thinking they walked in a straight line, had started to walk in circles. Some in small circles and some in larger ones, but everyone had walked in a circular fashion rather than straight. The final outcome of the research was simply this: when surrounded by darkness, man walks in circles.

I read about this and thought, "That is the history of mankind in a nutshell!"

Without the light of God, we walk in circles. Without the light of God, we keep repeating the same mistakes over and over again. Now, we may try to convince ourselves that we are making progress since we constantly invent new stuff. "Oh look, a new iPhone is out. We're going places!" But morally and ethically, we are going round and round. Five thousand years ago there were wars, crimes, inequality, and injustice. Today there are still wars, crimes, inequality, and injustice. Without the light of God, we walk in circles.

> We all, like sheep, have gone astray, each of us has turned to our own way.
>
> —ISAIAH 53:6

Picture a disconnected light bulb. I'm sure you have some spare ones in a cupboard somewhere in your house. This light bulb is created, beautifully and delicately, for one purpose alone: to shine, to light up its surroundings. However, if it was never connected to a power source (electricity), it would still exist yet be the most pathetic of inventions: something made for a purpose it never got to serve, something constructed for a need it never got to meet, something made for a task it never got to complete.

That is where we find ourselves as human beings without the light of God, and this is why we struggle so much to make sense of our reality. If wealth, celebrity, fame, and influence are the point and purpose of our existence, then why are so many of those who possess these qualities still on drugs, their marriages are still breaking down, and they are still committing suicide?

Answer: because it is really hard to find a new point of purpose for a light bulb if it has cut itself off from the electricity.

Ever since the Garden of Eden, this is where we have found ourselves. Created for light, yet disconnected from it by our own choices, we nonetheless try to convince ourselves that we are doing just fine on our own in the darkness, going round and round in circles, repeating our own historical mistakes and failures over and over again. We lie to ourselves that we don't need the light—that we are better off without it—even though our spirit, soul, and body tell us otherwise.

As Pharaoh in Egypt refused to let the people of Israel go, God punished him and his people by removing the light from Egypt.

> Then the LORD said to Moses, "Stretch out your hand toward the sky so that darkness spreads over Egypt— darkness that can be felt." So Moses stretched out his hand toward the sky, and total darkness covered all Egypt for three days. No one could see anyone else or move about for three days. Yet all the Israelites had light in the places where they lived.
>
> —EXODUS 10:21–23

Note the expressions used: "total darkness" so that "no one could move about." And especially "darkness that can be felt."

This is what we are experiencing in our societies today: a darkness, an absence of light that "can be felt." A desperate hopelessness and homelessness that society cannot cure, a deadly disease that cannot be healed in any way other than by returning to Him who is the light, thus returning to our true purpose: to live in the light of His presence and reflect His light wherever we go.

Praise God that even in this season of darkness, our Lord can still turn darkness into light (Ps. 18:28) and that the light still shines in the darkness—and the darkness has not overcome it (John 1:5)! Whatever darkness you might find yourself in, remember that "everyone who calls on the name of the Lord will be saved" (Rom. 10:13).

AN "ACCIDENTAL" UBER RIDE

A few years ago I was teaching on building a church for the next generation at a pastors' conference in Mexico City. About nine hundred pastors were gathered for the three-day event, and we had an amazing time in the presence of God.

Every morning of the event a new guy would pick me up and drive me to the church, and as we left the hotel behind on the third and final day of the conference, I started chatting with the driver and asked him about his family and work. We had a nice conversation, but when I asked him to tell me how he met Jesus, he suddenly grew silent on me. I could see that he was struggling and asked if he was all right, to which he replied, "Actually, no."

He then told me his life story—how he had been passionate for God as a child, how he was always at church, read the Bible, loved Jesus, and vowed as a teenager to live his whole life for the glory of God alone. But he had made a series of bad decisions, fallen for temptations, and gotten completely lost in life and in his relationship with the Lord. Remembering the holy promises he had made as a teenager and how radically he had broken them, he now assumed God must be disappointed and angry with him. How could he even think of approaching God after failing Him so horribly?

He cried like a baby as he shared his story, and I could feel his pain. Ever since leaving God's presence, he felt as if he had been in darkness in every area of his life. He had failed his parents, failed in love, failed at work, failed financially. Everything was just…dark.

In a silent prayer I asked for the help of the Holy Spirit then shared the gospel of light with him. I told him God was not disappointed or angry but was instead waiting for him with His arms open. I told him there was forgiveness, mercy, restoration, a new chance, and a new chapter available for him through faith in Jesus Christ—and that there could be light in his darkness. He cried even harder as I shared and had to pull the car off the interstate. I asked him if I could pray with him right then, and through his tears he looked at me and said yes.

We prayed, and I could almost feel the darkness and heaviness give way to light and joy. After having rededicated his life to Jesus, he was so relieved he laughed and cried for joy at the same time. The presence of God filled our small Volkswagen Beetle as the two of us sat rejoicing in the car, experiencing God turning darkness into light yet again.

After about fifteen minutes of praising God, however, I checked my watch and realized we were already very late for the conference sessions, so I asked him if we could get to the church as soon as possible. He looked back at me, puzzled, and said, "But we are going to the airport."

"No, no," I told him, "the airport is tomorrow. I have one more day left speaking at the conference in church. You have to get me there now!"

He looked at me again, and there was a weird moment of awkward silence in the car before he said something I will remember for the rest of my life:

"You are Mr. Williams, aren't you?"

And slowly it dawned on me: this was not my driver at all.

Turned out this guy was a random Uber driver who was supposed to pick up a Mr. Williams at my hotel at 9:45 a.m. and drive him to the airport. Nine forty-five was the exact time I was supposed to be picked up by a driver and taken to church. So when this guy showed up, I assumed he was my driver, he assumed I was Mr. Williams, and we headed off. And all was fine until "Mr. Williams" started asking him about his relationship with Jesus!

After he dropped me off at the church (and yes, I paid him), I had tears in my eyes as I watched him drive away. How much heavenly coordination had been invested in what had just happened? How many angels had been involved in keeping Mr.

Williams and my original driver away so that the two of us would meet and one more soul would be saved?

I had just been shown again how much God truly loves one single individual and what He is ready to do to bring one more human being out from the darkness and back into the glorious light we were all created to live in.

Chapter 4

PREPARING FOR THE
RETURN OF LIGHT

*W*E HAVE LEARNED that God Himself is light and that there is no darkness in Him. We have studied how He launched creation by first saying, "Let there be light," but also, tragically, how His own image—created to live in the light of His presence—ran away from Him and ended up in a darkness that still haunts the human race to this day.

This dramatic failure has absolutely nothing to do with God but was all an act of man's free will and choice. No one could blame God if He had simply turned His back on man at this point, said "Blame yourselves," and started over from scratch with a new universe and a new creation.

But His light and His love for you did not allow that. Instead He launched His master plan, one that would bring that lost light back into our dark world again. The light that, when turned on, would again cause miracles to happen and make the impossible possible.

Throughout the Old Testament God sent messengers to Israel, pointing toward a day when He would again proclaim, "Let there be light," and when the present darkness of man, caused by our own rebellion, would be turned back into glorious light:

> The moon will shine like the sun, and the sunlight
> will be seven times brighter, like the light of seven

full days, when the LORD binds up the bruises of his people and heals the wounds he inflicted.

—ISAIAH 30:26

I will turn the darkness into light before them and make the rough places smooth. These are the things I will do; I will not forsake them.

—ISAIAH 42:16

Then your light will break forth like the dawn, and your healing will quickly appear; then your righteousness will go before you, and the glory of the LORD will be your rear guard.

—ISAIAH 58:8

Arise, shine, for your light has come, and the glory of the LORD rises upon you. See, darkness covers the earth and thick darkness is over the peoples, but the LORD rises upon you and his glory appears over you. Nations will come to your light, and kings to the brightness of your dawn.

—ISAIAH 60:1–3

The sun will no more be your light by day, nor will the brightness of the moon shine on you, for the LORD will be your everlasting light, and your God will be your glory. Your sun will never set again, and your moon will wane no more; the LORD will be your everlasting light, and your days of sorrow will end.

—ISAIAH 60:19–20

Because I have sinned against him, I will bear the LORD's wrath, until he pleads my case and upholds

> my cause. He will bring me out into the light; I will
> see his righteousness.
>
> —MICAH 7:9

So even though the time was not yet right for the restorer of light to enter, God kept speaking about that day, pointing toward that goal, promising that even though we had broken the trust, failed His love, and left His light, He would bring that light back again and provide us all with a chance to leave our darkness behind.

These prophetic sparks of light kept appearing throughout the Old Covenant, as heralds of the day when the Light of the world would finally be revealed.

And God is still doing this today! We, His church, have been given the commandment to go into the whole world and share the good news of the gospel—that the light is now back and available for anyone who believes—but the Lord Himself is still highly involved in this process Himself.

HANDS LIFTED TO THE SKY

Let me tell you the story of one of the many Muslims who arrived in Sweden a few years ago during the great influx of refugees from the Middle East that I touched on earlier.

This young man, about twenty-five years old, had arrived in Sweden all alone and ended up in a city on the east coast, about an hour's drive north of Uppsala, where my church is. As he tried to adjust and acclimatize to this cold new home nation of his, he had a very strange experience: he started dreaming the same dream over and over again, every single night as he slept.

In the dream he saw a massive auditorium, and inside it, thousands of people standing with their hands lifted to the sky. Please remember that this young man was a Muslim. He had never experienced Christianity, had never visited a church in his life, and therefore had no idea what this auditorium was, who these people were, and why they all had their hands raised. The one thing he knew was that this sequence was played on repeat in his dreams every night.

Eventually he concluded that this experience had some kind of meaning. He could not interpret it any other way than that, for whatever reason, he was somehow supposed to find this mysterious auditorium. So he took to the streets of his new home city and started walking up to strangers asking, "Excuse me, can you help me find a huge auditorium where thousands of people stand around with their hands lifted to the sky?" On top of this being quite a strange request, Sweden is a very introverted nation where you hardly ever interact with strangers. Everybody assumed this young Muslim was crazy, and he got no help whatsoever in finding the mysterious place that kept showing up in his dreams.

He sat down to think. The auditorium appearing in his dreams was really big. Maybe it was located in a larger city than his. Maybe it was to be found in the capital of Sweden. What was it called...Stockholm?

The young Muslim bought a train ticket to Stockholm to try to track down the strange auditorium and find out why the people inside it had their hands lifted. And more than anything he wanted to find out why this scene kept popping up in his dreams.

Now, when you go by train from his home city to Stockholm, the last city you pass before arriving is Uppsala, where my church is located. So the young man passed by our city and soon after arrived at the Stockholm Central Train Station. As he exited the train, a complete stranger on the platform walked straight up to him. Contrary to the Swedish unwritten rule of not talking to strangers, this man told the young Muslim,

"Friend, you have gone one stop too far. You need to go back to the city prior to Stockholm, and you will find what you are looking for."

The Muslim, slightly confused, said thank you, got back on the train, and traveled back to the last train stop before Stockholm—the city of Uppsala—according to the directions of this stranger, who somehow seemed to know all about his mission. Once he arrived in our city, he took to the street again and walked up to the first available stranger, asking him where he could find a huge auditorium where thousands of people had their hands raised. "Oh, that's Word of Life Church," the stranger exclaimed. "Everyone knows that!"

Once the young Muslim had been given the directions, he got on a local bus and arrived at my church at about nine o'clock on this Saturday night. He went inside, realizing this was the first time he had even been inside a Christian church. As he entered the main auditorium, our service was in its final moment of worship, and the young man gasped at what he saw: this was the auditorium from his dreams!

He recognized everything—the balconies, the stage, the colors, the whole design.

And it was packed with thousands of people who had their hands raised to the sky.

The young Muslim stood there, watching in awe. Then he saw me come on stage, saying, "Maybe you are here tonight and you don't know Jesus." The young man listened intently. He heard the gospel of Jesus for the very first time. He realized he was in darkness and needed God's light, God's love, God's forgiveness, and when the altar call was made, he lifted his hand and accepted Christ into his heart.

It was only later, at the follow-up conversation, that we learned the amazing story that had brought him there in the first place: How God had given him a dream and put it on repeat. How he had been searching desperately to find this auditorium he didn't even know existed. How God had sent what must have been an angel to the Stockholm train station to push him in the right direction. And how God had made sure he found his way to our church at the exact moment of the invitation for people to accept Christ!

Just as God throughout the Old Testament pointed people toward the hope of the light returning to the world, He is still very much in the business of stirring and preparing hearts and leading them toward the Light of the world: Jesus Christ.

Chapter 5

JESUS—THE LIGHT OF THE WORLD

*E*VERYONE WAS WAITING.

The people of God were painfully aware of their position and its challenges. Man had gone astray, exchanging the light of God for the darkness of sin and rebellion. Still, they had heard the promises. The light would be brought back somehow. Their God would once again proclaim, "Let there be light," and once the light was on He would start the process of redemption, salvation, a new beginning.

But how? Though they had seen glimpses of the light throughout their history—the burning bush, the pillar of fire by night, the supernatural light that shone in their homes as darkness covered Egypt—they all knew the fullness of God's light could no longer dwell among them. The spiritual darkness of sin was found in every element of the human heart and soul, separating them forever from the glory of the Lord. They had heard it prophesied that a Messiah would bring the light back to them. But what kind of spiritual intervention would be powerful enough to remove the inner darkness of humans, restore man, and welcome him back into the presence of light?

A HUMBLE ENTRANCE

The time had now come for them to find out. Two thousand years ago, in God's perfect time, the seed of light was planted on earth.

> In him was life, and that life was the light of all
> mankind. The light shines in the darkness, and the

37

> darkness has not overcome it....The true light that
> gives light to everyone was coming into the world.
>
> —JOHN 1:4–5, 9

He made a humble entrance, initially observed by only two groups of people: the shepherds who suddenly saw the glory of the Lord shine down upon them from heaven on the slopes of Bethlehem the night of His birth (Luke 2:8), and the magi from the East who saw a shining star as a sign that the King, the Savior, was born (Matt. 2:1–2). Two manifestations of "Let there be light" announced to these two unexpected groups of people that with this child, the light of God would be making its way back to man.

What was the significance of these two groups being the first ones to worship? The shepherds represented the low, the poor, the simple people, and the magi represented the rich, the powerful, and the mighty. This child was sent to save them both, and everyone in between. He would be the light of the world for every man, at any level of society.

But even more significant: The shepherds were Jews. The magi were gentiles.

These two groups being the first to worship Jesus Christ, the Son of God, being born was a powerful, prophetic proclamation that this child was indeed the King of the Jews and the Savior of the seed of Abraham. But not only that. Through this baby boy, God would bring back the light to His covenant people and also to the entire world. The child would not only be the light of the Jews but the Light of the world!

After thirty years of preparation, it was time for this child, now a man, to step fully into the reason He was sent to earth. In the synagogue of the town where He grew up, He read the messianic promises from Isaiah:

> The Spirit of the Sovereign LORD is on me, because
> the LORD has anointed me to proclaim good news to
> the poor. He has sent me to bind up the brokenhearted,
> to proclaim freedom for the captives and release from
> darkness for the prisoners
>
> —ISAIAH 61:1

And then He added, "Today this scripture is fulfilled in your hearing" (Luke 4:21). This was His mission—to demonstrate the goodness and light of His Father and bring a "release from darkness for the prisoners."

This battle cry of His purpose would continue to sound through Israel:

> I am the light of the world. Whoever follows me will
> never walk in darkness, but will have the light of life.
>
> —JOHN 8:12

> I have come into the world as a light, so that no one
> who believes in me should stay in darkness.
>
> —JOHN 12:46

> There he was transfigured before them. His face
> shone like the sun, and his clothes became as white
> as the light.
>
> —MATTHEW 17:2

He truly is the Light of the world, sent to break the deadly circle of darkness and offer anyone who would come, anyone who would follow, to have the light of God restored!

And remember what we talked about in chapter 2?

When the light is turned on, God starts to work.

When the light is turned on, miracles will happen.

When the light is turned on, nothing is impossible.

Jesus is God's new covenant proclamation "Let there be light!" And the story from the dawn of creation now starts to repeat itself wherever He goes. With the light back on, God's creative power is once again released. The sick are healed, the possessed are delivered, the dead are raised, the sinners are forgiven, and those in darkness find light again.

In towns like Capernaum, where there was a genuine spiritual hunger and Christ was received, miracles abounded (Luke 8), but in other places, including Jesus' own hometown of Nazareth, He was met with an attitude of doubt and unbelief that prevented even Him, the Son of God, from shining the light and performing the miracles He longed to do (Mark 6). Even now, as the light of God is offered to anyone and everyone, it is still our free will—the same one we used to walk away from God and into darkness—that decides if we will receive or reject.

> Yet to all who did receive him, to those who believed
> in his name, he gave the right to become children of
> God.
>
> —JOHN 1:12

There is nothing more powerful, more beautiful, than seeing that divine transformation from darkness to light as the door of the human heart is opened and Jesus, the Light of the world, is allowed to enter. As I look back, my heart is warmed by all the times I've had the honor to be a spectator to this miracle. The first year after I gave my heart to Jesus at age sixteen, I shared the gospel and prayed for salvation with over thirty-five other young people in my town and fell in love with seeing the light come on inside them. I got to watch them experience the miracle of "Let there be light" and journey with them throughout those few first steps of their newfound life and future. It was amazing!

However, my strongest early memory of seeing light replace darkness occurred about one year after I had opened my heart to Christ. At that time, seventeen years old now, I heard a missionary named Carl-Gustaf Severin speak at a conference. He was making secret trips into the Soviet Union to smuggle Bibles in Russian and preach the gospel. This was before the collapse of Communism, and these activities were highly illegal since one of the ambitions of the Soviet Union for the previous seventy years had been to eradicate Christianity and keep the gospel as far away from its people as possible.

Carl-Gustaf's stories and testimonies of the spiritual hunger inside the Soviet Union fascinated me. I knew in my heart that I just had to see this for myself. After hearing him speak, I walked up to him, introduced myself, and asked if there was any way for me to come along with him the next time he made one of these mission trips. I would do whatever—carry his bag for him or anything. I just had to see and be a part of the revival going on there.

He said he would be happy to have me come along with him on a fourteen-day trip in a few months' time. Amazing news. Now I just had to get the money to pay for my ticket—I had absolutely none at the time. However, my high school graduation was coming up, and the Swedish tradition is that when a son or daughter graduates, the parents throw a big party and buy their graduate a nice gift.

This was my chance! I sat my parents down and told them I did not want a party or a gift. Instead I asked them to cancel all such plans and just give me the money they had planned to spend on my graduation so I could go to the Soviet Union with the missionary. It took some serious convincing, but they reluctantly agreed. The party and gift were canceled and I had a McDonald's meal for my graduation dinner, but who cared. I now had the money to go on my very first mission trip!

THROWN IN THE DEEP END

There is so much about this trip that I will never forget. One was looking out the window as our flight landed in Moscow. Though it was daytime, everything was dark, gray, and without color. Even the grass was gray rather than green. It was as if the curse of Communism and atheism was visible to the eye, and the spiritual darkness was so heavy and the light of God so shut out that the whole creation suffered. As we walked across the airport I did not see a single smiling face, nor a single color in the clothes of the people I passed. All was black, gray, worn, torn, dark, and depressed.

My missionary friends' contacts were waiting for us outside, quickly got us into a car, and sped off like crazy. The tires were screeching at every corner, and I asked my friend why they were going so insanely fast. He told me that the KGB, the Soviet secret police, were after us. I asked no more questions. I had watched loads of action movies growing up and now suddenly realized I was actually in one myself.

After a few hours of speeding out of the city and shaking off our followers, we arrived at a small house in a forested area, out in the middle of nowhere. As we stepped inside, I was shocked. Though it looked like a regular house from the outside, this was actually a secret, camouflaged church building with only one big room absolutely packed with people. The room would have been appropriate for about two hundred people but now housed at least eight hundred, all worshipping the Lord in Russian with loud voices and lifted hands. It was like stepping into another world, a parallel universe. All I had seen of the Soviet Union so far had been dark and depressing, but this was a celebration of light, joy, and impassioned love for Jesus. It was one of the most amazing things I have ever seen.

My missionary friend told me that many of the people had walked by foot for days to join the secret meeting that night. And the response they gave to the Word of God my friend preached was overwhelming. These people were starving, deprived for decades of the spiritual food their hearts needed and now finally had access to. Coming from the Western world where we are so incredibly spoiled by having constant access to all the Bible teaching we want at any time, this was a healthy wake-up call for me.

Carl-Gustaf preached for an hour, and when it was obvious that he was about to close the message, people actually started booing. They had walked for hours and risked their lives to get there and were not going to settle for just one hour of Bible teaching! So he had to start over with a second message, and one hour later, while coming to the end of it, the crowd again would just not have it. So he had no other choice than to start on a third one. When he was about to finish this now three-hour message, the crowd finally allowed him to, and he started to move into ministry time. I could see that he was really worn out from all the preaching, but I had no way to prepare for what would happen next.

"We are now going to pray for the sick," he proclaimed. The crowd cheered. "And my good friend Joakim will be the one praying for them!"

With that, he walked off stage and disappeared, probably to take a nap. And I now found myself alone, a seventeen-year-old with zero experience of praying for sick people, together with a passionate Russian crowd that *really* wanted to be prayed for. To say I panicked is an understatement. I had never done anything like this, only having seen other people pray for the sick. Still, I saw no way out of this situation. I was handed the mike and got up on stage, shaking but desperately pretending that I was in full control and knew what I was doing.

"Please come to the front if you're sick here tonight," I called out in my most "preachery" voice. Sweat was pouring down my back, and I hoped that just one or two would respond.

Instead, everyone in the room came to the front!

Since the place was packed, it felt as if an army had just taken a massive step forward. I turned to my interpreter and said, "No, no! I didn't ask for everyone to come up, just the sick ones." He replied, "Everyone is sick." This was the Soviet Union. No proper health care was available, and everyone had some kind of physical problem or two that they now wanted God to take care of.

So there I was with hundreds of people seeking prayer and no experience of praying for the sick. What if I messed up? What if I prayed the wrong way somehow and nothing happened? What if I needed a spiritual level of excellence I did not possess and ended up disappointing all these precious people?

A million thoughts whirled in my head as I walked up to the closest person in the crowd, a little Russian "babushka" lady, probably in her seventies or eighties. I tried to sound a hundred times more confident than I was while asking, through the interpreter, what was her problem. As a reply, she raised her left arm.

Honestly, this arm was like something out of a Japanese horror movie. It was the worst thing I had ever seen—like a skeleton arm covered by thin, gray skin. Her fingers were like tiny sticks, and it was obvious that she could not use this arm at all. And this was the first person I would ever pray for? God, couldn't we have started out with a headache or something?

The good thing, though, was that the situation made me realize there was absolutely nothing I could do to meet this need. This was certainly the place where Joakim Lundqvist came to an end and Jesus had to start. So I took her zombie hand in mine (and shivered as I did) and prayed the simplest and most desperate prayer ever: "God, heal her. Please!"

Then I looked at her arm. And during the course of some thirty seconds, my eyes witnessed the first miracle they had ever seen. I saw the arm slowly grow out to normal size, the gray get replaced with a healthy skin color, and the woman start to move her fingers.

She started screaming, laughing, and crying. I started screaming, laughing, and crying. Everybody started screaming, laughing, and crying! For the first time in my life I had seen with my own eyes the radical change of light replacing darkness. As the gospel of Jesus was preached in the spiritually darkest area I had ever experienced, and as its "Let there be light" was proclaimed, the power of God moved once again, performing miracles and making the impossible possible.

I will never forget that moment for the rest of my life. That entire mission trip, I smelled burning bridges behind me. I made up my mind in those two weeks that there was no way back for me now. All I wanted to do with the rest of my life was see this Jesus, the Light of the world, change the darkness of my world, my generation, into His beautiful, radiant light.

Chapter 6

YOU ARE THE LIGHT
OF THE WORLD

*W*ITH JESUS, THE light of God was now back on earth. Wherever He went, darkness was replaced by light, and as we know well by now, when the light is turned on, God starts working. In the footsteps of Jesus, the sick were healed, the oppressed delivered, and the dead raised. As the light came back on, the kingdom of God advanced all over Israel.

But one problem was still unsolved: Jesus, the Light of the world, was limited to His physical body. He could only shine God's light in one place at a time, and only those lucky enough to be in His physical presence would see it and experience its consequences.

God, however, knew exactly what He was doing, and everything was now slowly building up toward the most unexpected and amazing twist in the story of the light of God. Jesus Himself would reveal this part of God's great master plan as He looked out over the thousands of people listening to His teaching on the slope of Mount Eremos in Galilee:

> You are the light of the world.
>
> —MATTHEW 5:14

Wait, what?

Isn't Jesus the Light of the world? Isn't God the one and only source of the light that conquers darkness and enables His liberating power to move?

Yes.

And this God, and His light, is about to move into your

heart, thus allowing *you* to shine His light and bring it along wherever you go!

God's plan to bring His light back to earth would not be accomplished by Jesus walking into every nation, city, town, and village but by igniting His own light inside the hearts of millions of believers and have them go into the whole world and shine that same light.

> A town built on a hill cannot be hidden. Neither do people light a lamp and put it under a bowl. Instead they put it on its stand, and it gives light to everyone in the house. In the same way, let your light shine before others, that they may see your good deeds and glorify your Father in heaven.
>
> —MATTHEW 5:14–16

WE ARE LIVING PROCLAMATIONS

Let your light shine! This is the main calling of every believer in Jesus Christ: to be a living, breathing, walking proclamation of "Let there be light" to our families, friends, colleagues, fellow students, neighbors, and whoever we meet.

And when the light is turned on in our worlds, God will start to work.

It is so simple, yet we are world champions at getting it wrong. So many times we live out Christianity as if it were a way for us to get as much as possible out of life. We take the receiving end while God in fact sees us as the giving one. Truth is, we are not on this earth to fulfill our own desires and dreams but to shine God's light so that someone else can find his way out of darkness.

This truth is so obvious throughout the teaching of Christ, as in the parable of the woman and the lost coin.

> Or suppose a woman has ten silver coins and loses
> one. Doesn't she light a lamp, sweep the house and
> search carefully until she finds it?
>
> —LUKE 15:8

As the woman searches for the lost coin she "lights a lamp" to help her find it. It is quite obvious that the woman represents God and the lost coin is a lost soul without God's light. But what does that lamp represent then?

You.

In the search for yet another soul to save, another heart to fill with His Spirit, another life to bring out of darkness, God almighty "lights a lamp." He fills you with His light, takes you in His hand, and goes out to search. The focus of the story is not the lamp itself; it's all about finding the lost coin. But without the lamp that is you and me—"the light of the world," according to Jesus—the search will be so much harder and take so much longer.

> You are all children of the light and children of the
> day. We do not belong to the night or to the darkness.
>
> —1 THESSALONIANS 5:5

Let us never stop thanking God for this miracle! And let us never forget that this miracle happened for a reason. There is a purpose for your time on earth, a reason why God did not have you immediately raptured to heaven the second you accepted Jesus as your Lord and Savior: so that you could shine your light before others and be a lamp in the hand of the Almighty, enabling Him to find yet another lost coin.

So many will hear this and think, "But how could I ever shine the light with all my problems and imperfections? How in the world could someone ever see God's light through me?"

That is exactly what the enemy would love for you to think. When his main plan—to keep you away from the light of God— has failed and you have found salvation in Jesus, his alternative plan is to try to keep you in such a low level of spiritual confidence that you spend all your life looking at yourself as a renovation project that needs all the help it can get to simply survive. But in God's eyes you are the light of the world, a holy lamp in His hand, lit to help Him find another lost coin.

Let me remind you, the group of people that Jesus said was "the light of the world" was not an elite league of spiritual supermen. Quite the opposite. The Gospels tell us that "many tax collectors and sinners were eating with him and his disciples, for there were many who followed him" (Mark 2:15). You see, the light that shines from the "lights of the world" is God's light, not our own. Its origin is not our own perfection or self-righteousness but the presence of His Spirit inside us. That does not mean we should not constantly work on our holiness and make sure our lifestyle is in line with God's Word—not at all. But just as the light can shine inside a sinner from the first moment of salvation, it can shine through the sinner as well.

God chose "the foolish things of the world to shame the wise; God chose the weak things of the world to shame the strong. God chose the lowly things of this world and the despised things—and the things that are not—to nullify the things that are, so that no one may boast before him" (1 Cor. 1:27–29).

I want to share a beautiful testimony with you to emphasize this very truth, but first let me give you some context to fully understand it.

In Sweden, whenever a women gets pregnant, a special test called CUB is performed to reveal whether the child she is expecting has Down syndrome. If the test shows positive for Down syndrome, the vast majority of these babies are aborted. This is nothing less than an abomination and terrible proof that our society has become so self-centered and elitist that anything slightly outside the norm is not welcomed.

Also, what a cold, cruel message to send to the Down syndrome community, basically telling its members that "you should not even be here, and it was a mistake that you were born at all." I am not placing the full blame on the parents who make the decision to abort the pregnancy but also on our society as a whole. Instead of helping parents understand more about Down's, meet other parents of Down's kids, and providing support with what is needed to raise such a child, they are simply recommended the option of an abortion as the easy way out.

At my church, Word of Life, we have decided to be a counterculture to this spirit of death. We currently run eleven Christian schools in our city, and two of them are designed for children with Down syndrome or other special needs. Let us never forget that in the kingdom of God diversity is not a problem but an asset!

Also, who are we to say that one human life carries more worth than another? These children carry such a beautiful spirit of joy and happiness. Many times when I have had a tough day and felt a bit burdened, I have headed over to one of these two schools just to spend some time with this amazing group of children. And I have always left with a smile back on my face, always cheered up, always stirred in my spirit. Science claims that kids with Down syndrome have one chromosome too many, but sometimes I think it is the rest of us who have one too few.

SAVED BY A SONG

A few years ago, an eleven-year-old student with Down syndrome that attends one of these schools—let's call him John— was in the city center with his teacher for city training. This is where we teach the kids how to cross a street, how to make a purchase in a store, basically how to move about in a normal city environment.

As John and his teacher crossed the large open square that forms the center of Uppsala, John suddenly stopped and started singing. At the top of his voice.

Let me tell you, this is not normal behavior in Sweden by any means. People are very reluctant to stand out and become the center of attention, and certainly no one sings in public in an open square!

John kept singing this song that the teacher had never heard him sing before. "There is a tree in my garden that is a hundred years old," he sang as he kept up his loud solo performance in the square.

Less than a minute later, a woman came up to the teacher with tears running down her face. She grabbed the teacher by the arm, pointed at John, and asked, "Why is that boy singing that song?" To which the teacher could only reply, "I have absolutely no idea."

The woman then shared her story. She had been suffering from a long-term depression that had brought her to the point of not wanting to go on living, and she was now contemplating suicide. But that very morning, all alone in her apartment, she had prayed her first prayer ever to God.

"God, if You're out there, and if You care, please give me proof of Your existence and a sign that there is a reason for me to go on living. Let me hear that song today that was my favorite one when I was a little girl—the one about the tree in my garden that was a hundred years old."

A little later this woman crossed the main square of Uppsala, and as she passed by an eleven-year-old boy with Down syndrome, he heard the voice of the Holy Spirit. And this child—one that my nation doesn't even consider worthy to be alive—started singing a song that needed to be sung at that very second, becoming a lamp in the hand of the Almighty to find another lost coin.

This woman, having received the exact sign she asked for that morning through one of the most unexpected vessels, gave her heart to Jesus right there in the open square!

Later, when John was asked to sing the song again as the teacher retold the story, he couldn't do it. He did not know the song, neither before nor after this moment. But when the song needed to be sung to ignite the light of God and reach a lost soul, he could sing it.

My heart is warmed as I retell this story to you. The fact that God chose *the lowly things of this world*—the things this world will look down upon and expect nothing good from— speaks volumes about Him. And also, what was needed at that moment was not a parting of a sea or a calming of a storm but just the singing of a simple song—one that would ignite a light in the darkness for this woman. And when the light is turned on, God's power of salvation can start to work.

Let me tell you: if John, eleven years old with Down syndrome, could shine the light of God, so can you! You might not end up singing an unknown song in a square, but every single day provides you with endless opportunities to shine God's light to others.

In the upcoming chapters I will focus on the many ways you can be a light of your world, turn that light on wherever you go, and see God start working in your own world.

But like everything that involves God, the process is inside out, not the other way around. You did not become a new creation by wearing a cross necklace or a T-shirt that says "I believe in Jesus." Your sins were not forgiven by you trying really hard to change into a better person, thus deserving the grace of God.

Instead, your story of salvation started deep inside your heart, when you made the decision to accept what had been the will of God for you all the time, thus giving Him access to reach you, cleanse you from darkness, and save your soul. Then that salvation started working its way out to affect your character, your priorities, and your actions, words, and thoughts.

The same is true with becoming a true light in your world and shining for Jesus like never before. It doesn't start with your perfection or lack thereof; it's not a matter of gifts, talents, social skills, or personality.

Whoever you are, if Jesus is your Lord and His Spirit lives inside you, you can shine! If you want to.

If you do, why don't you just stop for a while, allow God's presence to surround you right now, and pray this prayer of commitment and surrender before reading on:

Lord, I thank You for being the God of light. Thank You for remaining faithful when I walked astray into the darkness, and thank You for sending Your Son, Jesus Christ, as the Light of my world. Thank You for shining the light of salvation into my heart, enabling me to have an unbroken relationship with You once again. And Lord, even though I know that I can do nothing in my own strength, I confess what You say about me:

I am the light of the world.

I am a lamp in Your hand.

I can shine the light of Jesus, and when the light is turned on, You will start to work in my world.

Thank You for being with me and shining through me today. In Jesus' name, amen.

PART II

TURN THE *Light* ON

*But you are a chosen people, a royal priest-
hood, a holy nation, God's special possession, that
you may declare the praises of him who called
you out of darkness into his wonderful light.*

—1 PETER 2:9

Chapter 7

TURN THE LIGHT ON—TAKE AN INITIATIVE, PART 1

*A*GAIN, THE BIBLE emphasizes that we have been called out of darkness into the light of God, not just to stay there but *that you may declare.* Jesus calls us the light of the world and then immediately adds that this light should not be restricted or put under a basket but allowed to shine to as many as possible. Why? So that when the light is turned on, God can start to work in the lives of the people in your world.

Now, for the upcoming chapters, let us focus on the next obvious question: How do we do this? How is the light turned on, and how can we shine for Jesus in our world?

First of all, we need to make it clear that shining does not happen automatically. When you accept Christ into your heart, you are born again, your sins are forgiven, and you become a child of God. However, you are not instantly turned into a world changer, though you are immediately given the potential to become one. Just as with your salvation, this is going to be an act of your free will connecting to the will of the Lord.

If we don't realize this, we will revert to a self-centered version of Christianity where we assume that our being used by God is all on His initiative and we have nothing to bring to the process: "If God wants to use me, He will." This is a very convenient approach since it implies that if I am not used by God—if my light doesn't shine for all to see—it's going to be God's fault, not mine. Yet this is not at all what the Word of God teaches.

RAISE YOUR STAFF!

Let's take a look at one of the most spectacular miracles of the Old Testament and how it came about.

As we enter the story, the children of Israel have just left the captivity of Egypt behind and started their journey back home to the Promised Land. However, though Pharaoh allowed them to leave, once they were gone he changed his mind and sent his army out to chase them down and bring them all back again. The Israelites now found themselves trapped between the Red Sea and the armies of Egypt.

> As Pharaoh approached, the Israelites looked up, and there were the Egyptians, marching after them. They were terrified and cried out to the LORD. They said to Moses, "Was it because there were no graves in Egypt that you brought us to the desert to die? What have you done to us by bringing us out of Egypt? Didn't we say to you in Egypt, 'Leave us alone; let us serve the Egyptians'? It would have been better for us to serve the Egyptians than to die in the desert!"
>
> Moses answered the people, "Do not be afraid. Stand firm and you will see the deliverance the LORD will bring you today. The Egyptians you see today you will never see again. The LORD will fight for you; you need only to be still."
>
> —EXODUS 14:10–14

Moses' reaction is understandable. He doesn't have the exact answer as to what will happen, but he tries his best to calm the people down and encourage faith in God. So far, well done.

But then he ends his faith-stirring speech with an interesting sentence: "The Lord will fight for you; you need only to be still." This is a verse I have seen on countless Christian posters, heard in worship songs, and read in devotionals. And you can easily understand why, as it takes a very comfortable approach to whatever problem we face. God will solve it for me. I don't have to do anything at all. I'll just relax with a cup of coffee and ask God to give me a call when He's done.

Now, I don't want you to misunderstand what I am saying: there are other scriptures—for example Psalm 37:7, Psalm 46:10, Zechariah 2:13—where the Lord Himself does encourage us to be still. But these verses are about being still in His presence, being still enough to hear Him, being still enough to get to know Him better. In the Exodus story, however, Moses seems to suggest that since we can't do anything about the situation we are in, we'll just hand the full responsibility over to God while we take the positions of passive spectators.

But God isn't having that at all. Look at His instant reply to what Moses just said:

> Then the LORD said to Moses, "Why are you crying out to me?"
>
> —EXODUS 14:15

This is a very unusual comment to come from God. Normally He is all in favor of us calling out to Him, and He encourages us to do so. But there seems to be something about the way Moses called out that displeased Him this time. What might that have been? Let's read on.

> Tell the Israelites to move on. Raise your staff and stretch out your hand over the sea to divide the water so that the Israelites can go through the sea on dry ground.
>
> —EXODUS 14:15–16

Hmm. So Moses claimed, "The LORD will fight for you; you need only to be still." To which God replied, "Why are you crying out to Me? Raise your staff and stretch out your hand over the sea to divide the water."

It is all becoming clear now. God was not comfortable with Moses taking a position where he expected God to do everything while he himself watched from a balcony seat. God wanted Moses to take an initiative that He could bless, one that He could magnify and multiply.

The miracle God wanted to perform would be a collaboration between God and man, where man's contribution would be a tiny, insignificant, and seemingly insufficient initiative, which in the eye of the Lord would be a light switch. A small step of faith would turn on the light, and—remember?—when the light is turned on, God starts to work!

Look at what happens:

> Then Moses stretched out his hand over the sea, and all that night the LORD drove the sea back with a strong east wind and turned it into dry land. The waters were divided, and the Israelites went through the sea on dry ground, with a wall of water on their right and on their left.
>
> —EXODUS 14:21–22

The waters were not divided and God's power was not released until Moses took the small step of faith that was lifting his staff and stretching out his hand over the sea. Surely he must have looked at that staff, then at the sea, then at the staff again, thinking to himself, "How in the world is this staff going to make any difference whatsoever?" And he would have been right! The only thing he held in his hand—all he could bring to the table—was totally insufficient as a solution to the problem.

This is why so many times we see so little of God's power released. We look at our own resources, our own staff, compare it to the challenges we are facing, and realize that whatever I can do will not be enough anyway—and then take the approach of "The Lord will fight; I am just gonna be still."

But God did not ask Moses to solve the problem, nor does He ask you to. He asked Moses to provide Him with an initiative of faith. He asked Moses to flick a little switch so that the light would come on, and then God would do the rest.

So back to the original question: How do we turn the light on? How can we shine for Jesus? The first answer is: by taking an initiative, a small step of faith that in God's eyes will be a spark of light, which is all He needs to start working.

We see this principle throughout the Bible. First Moses lifts his staff, then God divides an ocean. First Joshua's army lifts a shout of faith, then God brings the walls of Jericho down. First Elisha strikes the Jordan River with the mantle, then God dries it up. First the woman with the issue of blood grabs hold of the mantle of Jesus, then God heals her. First Peter and John take the hand of the paralyzed man by the Beautiful Gate, then God heals him.

None of these people could take any of the glory for the end result. That belonged to God and God alone. Still, none of these miracles would have happened if they had refused to provide God with that small initiative He could bless and magnify—that sparkle of light that would release His creative power.

We also see this principle of the small initiative repeatedly throughout human history, well into modern times. Let me tell you one out of thousands of stories.

THE MONTGOMERY BUS BOYCOTT

It's December 1, 1955. The sun is rising over the rooftops, and an African American pastor sits in his kitchen drinking his morning coffee. He is content with his life, as many of his dreams and ambitions have been fulfilled even at the early age of twenty-five. Like his father, he has studied to become a pastor and now has a permanent position at a church in Montgomery, Alabama. He has found a wonderful wife and been blessed with his first child, a daughter, Yolanda Denise, who is asleep in her cradle on the upper floor, not even two weeks old.

So it is with great satisfaction that he skims through the newspaper this Thursday morning—until the moment when his eyes fall on a certain picture. It is taken from inside a bus, empty except for a Black woman and a seemingly annoyed White man in the seat behind her. The pastor reads the story and is once again reminded that society is not as harmonious as life within his own four walls.

The woman was a certain Miss Rosa Parks, forty-two years old. The picture was taken when she was on her way home from work on a bus that was as full as buses in Montgomery always were at that time of day. The text further explained how the White man in the picture had stepped on the bus, walked up to Miss Rosa, and claimed her seat for himself in accordance with the segregation rules stating that Black people were obliged to give up their seats for Whites. But Miss Rosa Parks had had enough. For the first time in her life her patience was gone. No, she was not going to move. No, she was not going to leave her seat. She had worked hard all day. She was a woman. And she was there first!

The situation started to take on enormous proportions. The bus stopped, and all the other passengers had to get out and find other buses. Miss Rosa refused to move, and the man refused to take any other seat in the bus except for hers alone, even though all the other seats were now available. The police were called, and the picture in the newspaper was taken while Rosa was still in her seat, soon to be arrested for offensive behavior.

The pastor reads the article thoroughly. Then he reads it again. It is not the first time he has become aware of the injustice and unrighteousness in his society, but it is the first time he realizes that he personally has to do something. He doesn't have a clue about exactly what. He has no influential contacts, no friends with high-level political jobs, no education in the law—he is just your average pastor. But somehow these excuses are too thin now. He can't hide behind them. This is his responsibility, his society, his people.

Inspired by a woman who dared to say no to injustice at the price of her own convenience, he starts to think hard. What, what, what can he do? Not in a few years but here and now. Today.

He calls a few other pastor colleagues, and together they meet, pray, and talk. After some time they reach a conclusion. They agree on a simple action that if successful could at least be a small indication that there are actually people around who don't accept the racist laws. They agree that this upcoming Sunday they will encourage their congregations to boycott the buses of Montgomery on Monday morning and walk to work instead, or share spaces in the few cars available in their community. That way, if enough people join in, they can openly show their dissatisfaction.

The plan is set into motion, the call is made at a few churches in the Sunday services, and on Monday morning the young pastor and his wife sit by their kitchen window waiting for the first morning bus to pass by. They nervously agree that if there are about 30 percent fewer passengers on the bus than usual, the action has been successful. They hear the first bus approaching at a distance, and when it passes their house they see that it is...completely empty. The next one passes by. Empty. The next. Empty.

Then they look down on the sidewalk that used to be empty this time of day and see something beautiful beyond belief: a broad stream of people who are walking to work. Not depressed, miserable, and complaining, but singing and rejoicing with the unique joy you get when you know you are doing the right thing, even if it is not the most convenient.

Black people and White people side by side, singing joyous worship songs with their eyes full of pride and triumph.

The Montgomery bus boycott of December 5, 1955, stirred souls in a way no one thought possible. Now nobody wanted this to be a onetime event. No way! People wanted to continue walking to work every day until the segregationist bus laws were changed in the whole state. Energy and motivation were released like never before in people who had previously just accepted the situation.

People organized car sharing and helped each other out. They had prayer meetings, drew strength from their faith and church communities, and got involved in every kind of way. Day after day thousands of people refused traveling on the buses, instead standing up for what was right. Finally, after a full year of walking to work, the bus companies surrendered and changed their racist regulations.

An initial goal had been reached, but now something had been set in motion that could not be stopped. The initiative in Montgomery had inspired thousands of people throughout the state and other parts of the nation, and marches and demonstrations, always peaceful and free of any violence, were organized in one place after another.

The young pastor was invited to Birmingham, Alabama— at the time the most racist city in the state—where students wanted to hold a demonstration against the ungodly laws of segregation. Two thousand youths signed up for the planned action. Even though they knew they could very well end up in jail, they marched together into the parts of the city center that were reserved for White people only. They were met by police dogs, water guns, and batons. Many students were arrested and put in jail, so many that the jails were overflowing and news about the event was broadcast all over the country—which was exactly what the pastor had planned!

The White House began to take action and question the laws of Alabama, and tens of thousands in state after state were inspired to take similar stands for what was right rather than for what was comfortable and easy.

On August 28, 1963, almost eight years later, pastor Martin Luther King Jr. stood before a quarter of a million people in Washington, DC, at the greatest US demonstration to date and held one of the most famous and important speeches of his century: "I Have a Dream."

Many look at that occasion and think, "Wow, what a great leader! What an amazing man!" And I would certainly agree and join in with any praise given to his life and legacy.

But let us not forget that this whole nationwide movement really started with an ordinary woman named Rosa Parks, who made a decision on board an ordinary bus and decided to do what was right instead of what was easy. To start where she was. To use what she had. To lift a staff.

And in the eyes of God, she flicked a light switch.

Because when the light comes on, through a small initiative of faith, God will always start to work.

Chapter 8

TURN THE LIGHT ON—TAKE AN INITIATIVE, PART 2

*L*IFT YOUR STAFF. Use what is in your hand right now. Take an initiative.

It is so simple that we tend to miss it again and again, thinking we need to be pros and perfect to be used by God. As if He would be in need of our talents and resources. He isn't. He just needs that initiative, that small step of faith. He just needs for you to flick that light switch.

Over and over we place the responsibility for the expansion of God's kingdom on someone else—the pastor, the evangelist, the church staff, and basically anybody else within a five-mile radius—and simply assume that we are not qualified to participate in the process ourselves.

Gradually, we are turned into disconnected light bulbs, created to shine but having believed the lie that we can't. And so we have instead comfortably placed ourselves in the box in the cupboard.

This leaves us frustrated and dissatisfied, and since we are not busy doing what we were created to do, we take the frustration out on our Christian brothers and sisters. We start fighting over small matters, building up barriers between denominations and feeling threatened by the success of others. We whine for years because somebody stepped on our toes and dig deep into things that no one outside our own little isolated group couldn't care less about. We stop shining the light, God is left without our initiatives, and the world stays dark around us.

Soon our souls start to shrink and our joy disappears.

Instead of shining our lights, working together to build up God's kingdom in our world, we construct a Christian entertainment culture and life becomes a lookout for the coolest Christian event with the coolest Christian it-guy speaking. Our focus is no longer on finding the lost coin but on distancing ourselves from the world, judging sinners who don't know any better, spreading conspiracy theories online, and becoming known as a cult of angry, judgmental, isolated pharisees rather than the lights of the world.

I call this SBS—spiritual bedsore syndrome. Bedsores are something I came in painful contact with when I served in the Swedish army and was assigned the medic of my platoon. During my basic training I had to complete four weeks of practical experience in a hospital. Since I was the new kid on the block, the nurses had me do their least favorite task, which was taking care of the patients with bedsores. These are sores which older people or people not able to move will get on their heels, shoulders, or neck from lying still in their beds, often after major surgeries. Since they are unable to get up and walk around, their skin wears against the bed, and as a result oozing sores appear that smell terrible.

I believe the exact same thing happens spiritually when Christians do not realize we are called to be lights in the world, when we lose our focus on reaching the lost, and when we never give God initiatives to bless and multiply. We get spiritual bedsores from simply lying down too much and not moving about the way we should. Our introverted Christian lives begin to scab up, and after a while they produce pus and smell bad. So bad, in fact, that even the world outside can smell it.

The good news is that change is coming, and you can be part of it!

I thank God for what I have seen happening across the world in these last few years. There is a new generation of all

ages rising up that wants to do everything in their power to
erase that negative image of Christians. One that isn't satisfied
by only hearing about Jesus in church on Sunday morning but
is determined to do anything in their power to see the light of
God spread across their world. And one that is ready to start
the process by giving God whatever initiative is needed for His
power and love to be launched into their reality.

CAN WE TRUST THESE KIDS?

Personally, I have never seen the principle of turning the light
on by taking an initiative any clearer than when we launched a
movement called New Generation in Sweden. The backstory is
that for many years I had been struggling about how to reach the
schools of my nation with the gospel of Jesus and the love of God.

Since Sweden is one of the most secularized nations in
the world, schools were 100 percent off limits for any kind of
Christian activity. There was no chance for us as a church to
run any kind of program there or even physically enter a school
building.

Still, I knew that schools are the most important places in
society to reach. School is the one place that the entire future
nation has in common. Tomorrow's prime minister, tomorrow's
prostitute, and everyone in between will, for a few years, be in
the same room together before they are split up into all the different levels and layers of society. If we could reach them for
Jesus while they were there, we could reach the entire future of
our nation! But how could we if we were not even allowed inside?

And then a new vision from God dawned in my heart: What
if we just trusted the young people themselves, the Christian
students in the schools, to take initiatives for God and turn on
the light in their own schools? What if we as a church did not
take the approach of being the doers but rather the supporters

of the teenagers themselves, encouraging them and believing for them to flick the light switch of their own world and see God start working?

It sure sounded risky enough. Could we really trust fourteen-year-olds and sixteen-year-olds with doing God's work? What if they messed it up? What if they did a lot of crazy things that would bring shame to the reputation of Jesus and Christians?

But then all these stories from the Bible came back into my mind: how God called a young Mary to be the mother of His Son (Luke 1), a young Jeremiah to prophesy in His name (Jeremiah 1), a young David to be the best king Israel ever had (1 Samuel 16), a young Joshua to lead the people of God into the Promised Land (Joshua 3), a young Samuel to be the greatest man of God in his time (1 Samuel 3).

And I realized that if God dared to trust in all these young people, so should we!

Said and done, we got a basic concept together and encouraged our young people to start student-run New Generation groups in their school, gathering all Christians but not for the sake of debating theology among each other or even to run internal Bible studies to edify themselves, but to do two things only: pray for school revival and reach the students with the gospel of Jesus.

Little did I know when we launched New Generation that this would turn into the fastest-growing youth movement—Christian or secular—in the entire nation. Little did I know that hundreds of New Generation groups would start across Sweden and stir such a fresh wave of joy, passion, prayer, and evangelistic creativity. Little did I know that this movement would bring students from every Christian denomination together, not centered on celebrating the Lord's Supper in the exact same way but on winning souls in their schools for Christ.

On the night of New Generation's initial launch, when I was

about to preach this vision for the very first time to thousands of teenagers at Word of Life's annual Youth Conference, I had already prayed that we would soon hear testimonies about groups being started, initiatives being taken, and young people getting saved. Stories that we would be able to retell, inspiring others to do the same thing. In my mind I saw these initial testimonies potentially coming from university groups where Christian students would have the strength, courage, and spiritual maturity to reach others for Jesus.

But what happened was something completely different from what I had expected.

The first person that signed up that night to start the first New Generation group ever in Sweden was anything but that bold, mature university student. It was a small, scared-to-death twelve-year-old girl named Jannie. She happened to be at the conference, and when she heard about the launch of New Generation and how God wanted her to be a light of her world, of her school, her heart was stirred. Still, her mind screamed *no*!

Jannie had never seen herself as a leader. She was quiet, shy, and not outspoken or outgoing at all. She was a Christian, for sure, but would never really be seen or heard. As far as she knew, she was the only Christian in her school. And she had never shared Jesus with anyone. How would she muster the courage to take this kind of initiative? But her heart kept pounding, and eventually she gave in. She made up her mind that, yes, she would start a New Generation group on the Monday when she was back in school. She didn't know how she would dare to do it, but she would.

What Jannie didn't know was that this small decision—this tiny initiative in the heart of a shy Swedish girl—became, in the eyes of God, a staff lifted and a light switch being flicked. The light had been turned on, and God was getting ready to start working.

MIRACLE AT THE BUS STOP

On the Monday Jannie was back in school, she was dead-scared but committed to follow through on the decision she had made. She didn't know a single soul in the school who would be interested in joining a Christian group, but she did not let that stop her. Shaking, sweating, and going completely against her personality, she put up a poster on the school information board welcoming anyone to join the New Generation gathering that upcoming Friday. There. At least she had done something. At least she had taken a small initiative.

Once classes came to an end that Monday, Jannie went to the bus stop to catch her ride home. While waiting for the bus, however, she spotted another girl standing nearby, crying. As I've pointed out, Swedes are very introverted with their feelings, so seeing someone crying in public is very rare, and Jannie didn't know how to handle this situation. Her personality and the Swedish standard way of behaving both told her to look the other way, mind her own business, and hope the bus would be there very soon. But again, her heart started pounding. She remembered she had promised Jesus at the conference that she would be a light of her world—that she would shine His love on anyone who needed it.

After a few minutes of an internal civil war between her heart and her personality, Jannie took a deep breath and walked up to the crying girl, asking if she was all right and if there was anything she could do to help. Though Jannie was a complete stranger, the girl opened up and while sobbing shared how her whole world was falling apart. Her parents were filing for divorce, her best friend had left her, she was failing at school—everything was just pitch-black.

Jannie took another deep breath and said, "I know someone who can help you." For the very first time in her life, she shared the gospel she had always believed in but had never communicated. As she did, she was surprised at how much she really knew. It was as if everything she had heard from her parents, in kid's church, and at youth meetings came alive and made sense. The girl listened, asked questions, wanted to know more. Buses arrived and left, but the girls didn't care—they stood at the bus stop talking for hours. Finally, Jannie invited the girl to come over to her house, and that night the girl accepted Jesus as her Lord and Savior.

The story didn't end there either. During that same week, little twelve-year-old Jannie, who had never told anyone about Jesus before, got to lead four more girls at her school to faith in Jesus. When one of our mentor teams visited her city just a few months later and asked how things were going with her New Generation group, she answered, "It's going great! Now I've got fifteen!" The team were impressed, knowing that Jannie had started from scratch, and commented, "Wow! Fifteen students in the group already?" To which Jannie replied, "No, no! I mean fifteen *leaders!*"

It turned out that in these past few months alone, some sixty to seventy students had accepted Christ through the testimony of Jannie and her New Generation group. She had now had to train the first fifteen converts to become leaders alongside her to spearhead the revival and take care of all those who were getting saved!

God had proved me wrong. The spreading of the gospel in the schools and universities of Sweden would not be down to elite Christian students, the kind of people who were basically born with a King James Bible and a preacher's haircut. This movement would instead be characterized by ordinary, day-to-day young people—many times feeling scared, insignificant, and unqualified—but who nonetheless chose to identify as lights in their world and dared to take an initiative for God,

flick the light switch in their schools, and simply take the position of Isaiah: "Here am I, send me."

It was not the testimonies of strong and brave people but of
young ones like Jannie that allowed New Generation to grow
into a movement of some fifteen thousand Swedish students and
twenty-five thousand across Europe, united in a battle cry to see
God's kingdom invade the schools and universities of their nations.

To me, this is a perfect example of what being a light of the
world is really all about, and it also shows the nature of God's
entire kingdom. It is all about what Paul wrote in 1 Corinthians,
the first chapter:

> Brothers and sisters, think of what you were when you
> were called. Not many of you were wise by human
> standards; not many were influential; not many were
> of noble birth. But God chose the foolish things of the
> world to shame the wise; God chose the weak things
> of the world to shame the strong. God chose the lowly
> things of this world and the despised things—and the
> things that are not—to nullify the things that are, so
> that no one may boast before him.
>
> —1 Corinthians 1:26–29

Thank God for full-time ministers, pastors, preachers, and
leaders in the kingdom. But we will never see God's power of
salvation fully released in our cities and nations until we all
come to the same place Jannie did: realizing that even though
she felt too small, too weak, and too inexperienced, she could
still shine the light by taking an initiative for God in her own
world and reality.

And let me tell you: If she could do it, you can do it!

Chapter 9

TURN THE LIGHT ON—
START TO PRAY

*T*HE STORY OF the day of Pentecost is well known, especially among Spirit-filled Christians, and for good reasons. Not only is it an amazing, beautiful story in itself, but we also know it was the launching pad—the birthday—of that remarkable entity Jesus had promised would conquer even the gates of hell: the church.

Yet many times as we approach the story, we look at it as though the outpouring of the Holy Spirit happened 100 percent on God's initiative, disconnected from the disciples in the Upper Room. But when we read closely, we see that this turns out to be yet another one of the many biblical examples of a cooperation between God's great power and man's small initiative. The followers of Jesus were not sitting passively in the room, waiting for God to do something. They did not take the "you need only to be still" approach, praise God. Instead we read:

> They all joined together constantly in prayer, along with the women and Mary the mother of Jesus, and with his brothers.
>
> —ACTS 1:14

The Upper Room was not a place of sitting around waiting for God to make His move; it was a place of constant praying, of calling out to God together to fulfill His promises and for Him to pour out the power they needed to fulfill the Great Commission. Even though Jesus had promised this would

75

happen, they still prayed constantly and fervently for the promise to be fulfilled.

When God saw this group of people praying, His eyes saw them flicking the light switch. And when the light came on, God started to work, the Spirit was poured out, and the world would never be the same again.

To this day, prayer is and always will be one of the best ways to turn the light on. And the beautiful thing about prayer is that you can pray anywhere, at any time, and at any age. Some prayers are powerful proclamations of God's Word; some are silent whispers for help. Some come from hearts mature through decades of walking with the Lord; some from hearts that were just filled with His love for the very first time only seconds ago. Some are long, some are short. Some loud, some silent. Some read, some spontaneous. But every single prayer that comes from an honest heart is a light switch in God's eyes—an initiative saying, "Let there be light in my life and in my world." And this is just what God needs and exactly what He might well have been waiting for all along.

Your prayers release the light of God!

This is why all hell shakes when a Christian prays and why the devil is doing whatever he can to keep you away from doing so by telling you it's not worth it, nothing will happen anyway, and you're not good enough to get your prayers answered. Because he knows that should you start praying, the light will come on, and that would be the beginning of the end to his kingdom of darkness.

Madeleine's Prayer "Hit List"

Some years ago a sixteen-year old girl called Madeleine heard me speak on prayer, stating that God's light is turned on as we pray. She was one of many Christian young people who didn't really pray much at all, apart from the common prayers at the youth meetings and Sunday services of her church. But Madeleine walked back home that day with a newfound commitment to start praying. Not just general prayers but specific ones; not just for her own needs but for those who really seemed to need the light of God more than most.

To bring structure and plan into her prayers, Madeleine came up with quite a unique prayer pattern. She made a list of the ten worst bullies in her high school, those who terrorized the school halls and whom the other students feared, and especially those who made fun of her and bullied her for being a Christian (which happens a lot in Sweden). She ranked the list so that the worst bully of them all made number one, the second worst number two, and so on, and she made up her mind that she would pray for name number one on the list— the worst bully of them all—every day until he accepted Jesus as his Lord. Once that happened, she would start praying for name number two and go on until that person surrendered to Christ, and then work her way down the list in the same fashion.

Please note: I am not talking about a professional intercessor here but of a regular teenage girl with hardly any prior experience of private, personal prayer. Madeleine was pretty much the only believer in Jesus at her school, which is also the reality for many Christian young people, so there was no group support of her brand-new conviction. This was just an ordinary girl making a small, personal decision to pray for a few minutes by herself every morning that salvation would come to a lost soul.

But in God's eyes, this was more than just a few minutes of prayer. This was the flicking of a light switch.

The name at the top of Madeleine's list of bullies was Nils. He was a rebel, a known bully, and especially one that hated all things Christian. He had no interest at all in God and did not believe in Him one bit. Always quick to torment Madeleine for being a Christian, he had no idea he'd just become the target of her prayers. Every morning she called out to God to save Nils, forgive Nils, and show His love to Nils.

"Every morning I pointed my prayer bazooka at him!" Madeleine told me later. I did not even know there was such a thing as a prayer bazooka, but apparently you learn a lot from teenagers.

As the days and weeks passed, Nils started to feel a bit uneasy. He didn't understand why he had started to think about God and Jesus all the time. He did not want to. None of his friends brought up that topic. Sweden is completely secularized, so neither the media nor school nor society as a whole would naturally say anything at all about God. So why was Jesus the first thing on his mind every morning when he woke up? Why did God show up in his mind throughout the day and even in his dreams at night? Was he going crazy?

After months of struggling with these weirdly recurring thoughts about Jesus, Nils finally decided to put God to the test. All alone in his apartment, he prayed his very first prayer to the God he did not believe in, challenging Him to prove His existence.

"God, if You're out there somewhere, show Yourself to me. Give me a sign of Your existence: make me vomit!"

This is the stupidest prayer I have ever heard of in my life. I'm thinking to myself, "Why, Nils, why? Out of all the things you could have prayed for, 'make me vomit,' really?"

Well, well. As we know, God is a good God who answers our prayers so that our joy will be fulfilled. It took two seconds, and Nils' answer of prayer was on its way. All of a sudden he found himself running to the bathroom, humbly going down on his knees, and—let's just say that everything within him came out.

When later telling me about this experience, Nils said: "You know, sometimes you can get that strong, sudden reaction when you've eaten something bad. But that normally goes away in like twenty or thirty minutes. This thing, however, went on for twelve hours!"

I thought to myself, "Our God sure is El Shaddai, the God that is more than enough…"

After twelve hours of being sick, Nils finally realized this experience must be a direct answer to prayer, God's own proof of His existence in exactly the way Nils had asked for. So he prayed his second ever prayer in life: "God, if You're out there—make this stop!"

It stopped immediately. Nils crawled to bed and slept for twelve hours solid. He then woke up and gave his heart to Jesus. Back in school he told Madeleine of his experience, and the two of them started praying for name number two on the list.

After only six months, Madeleine and her new friends were down to praying for name number eight on the list—the seven worst bullies of her school had all accepted Jesus as their Lord and Savior!

Now obviously God had wanted to save these bullies all the time. In 1 Timothy 2:4 we read that God "wants all people to be saved and to come to a knowledge of the truth." But before that could happen, He needed someone to take the initiative of prayer, someone to lift a staff, someone to turn on the light so that His creative power could be released.

Prayers are not answered through perfection. If Jesus lives inside you, you have the ability to pray and be heard by the Almighty. So start where you are right now. If you don't pray much, or never, there is no need to try to soothe your bad conscience by making big promises and huge proclamations that "from now on I will pray four hours every morning." You will just fall asleep ten minutes into that first session, then wake up, feel even worse about yourself, and be even more reluctant to take another initiative of prayer.

Instead, if you are at square one of prayer, start by committing to thirty seconds of prayer every morning. But make sure you are not just praying for your own personal emergency needs. Pray for someone else. Get involved in praying for those around you that need Jesus in their lives: relatives, neighbors, fellow students, friends, colleagues at work. Make lists of people, and keep mentioning them in prayer. As you do, remember that you are doing so much more than just speaking words. You are lifting a staff over the Red Sea. You are giving God an initiative to bless and magnify. You are turning on the light. And you will see that those initial thirty seconds will grow and grow as the days go by.

While we are on the subject of prayer, I have to tell you about a twenty-one-year-old guy I met in Russia many years ago as my church started the work that has now led to over three hundred Word of Life churches planted in that nation. He and a group of his friends were breakdancing at a youth conference where I was speaking, and as I met up with them after the service, he told me his story.

FLIPPING THE LIGHT SWITCH IN THE URALS

The young man was from the Ural mountain area of Russia, and a few years earlier he and some of his Christian friends from other parts of Russia had traveled to attend a Swedish youth conference where I preached about turning on God's light by taking an initiative of prayer. This guy was in his teens at the time and never assumed that he could be used by God or, even less, that God would need him and his initiative.

After the conference he went back to his town in Ural,

determined to take some kind of initiative and see something happen. The challenge was that he was now totally alone. All his Christian friends lived in other cities far away, and there was not even one Christian church in his own city. But this guy, nineteen years old at the time, would not let anything stop him.

He began to do prayer walks around town late at nights. As he walked around, he saw the youth partying and living far away from God, and he prayed for their salvation. He did this every night.

Then one evening he saw another teenager breakdancing outside a bar. He knew the guy was on drugs and funded his addiction through dancing. When he was done performing, the nineteen-year-old walked up to him and shared Jesus with him. Every night he came back, stood there praying until the breakdance guy was done, and then again walked up and told him about Jesus. After many nights of praying and sharing, he finally got to lead the dancer to faith in Christ.

Not long after this, again as a result of prayer, he also saw the power of God break the chains of addiction over this young dancer and totally set him free. The transformed young dancer then brought five of his friends to the nineteen-year-old, all of them involved in drugs, criminality, and prostitution. Soon all of them had accepted Christ, and their lives were totally trans-formed by God's power, forgiveness, and love.

Together, this group of young people put together a break-dance act to share their newfound faith with others. They started dancing in streets and squares, schools and youth cen-ters. Hundreds of young people watched them dance and heard their testimonies, and many decided to become Christians themselves.

When all this happened, the now twenty-one-year-old guy told me, "We had a bit of a problem because there was no Christian church in the city. So I started one! I thought, 'Well, how hard can it be?' And now the church is full of people who have been saved by Jesus since."

I could hardly believe my ears.

"And how many is that?" I asked him.

"Six hundred and fifty. And our building can take just a bit more than two hundred, so we're now doing three services every Sunday and are about to start a fourth!'"

In a town in the Ural region of Russia that previously did not even have a Christian church, a full-blown revival had started, launching a nineteen-year-old guy into a twenty-one-year-old pastor of 650 newly saved souls, many of them former drug addicts, criminals, and prostitutes.

Who did all this? God.

Who should get the glory for it? God and God alone.

How could it happen? Because a regular teenage guy decided to cooperate with God and turn on the light so that His creative power could be released and make all things new.

That same God is waiting for someone to pray and take an initiative in every part of the world so that His power can start moving.

That is how His will is done, that is how His kingdom will come.

Chapter 10

TURN THE LIGHT ON—
SHOW GOD'S LOVE

$\mathcal{S}$O WE HAVE already stated that we can bring the light back into our worlds by giving God an initiative He can bless and magnify, and also by praying for the people around us to see the light of salvation.

Let us add one more thing to the list, and this is such an important one: we turn on the light in our world by showing God's love.

> In the same way, let your light shine before others,
> that they may see your good deeds and glorify your
> Father in heaven.
> —MATTHEW 5:16

In this verse, one of our key references so far, Jesus clearly states that the light within us is not something that others will mysteriously experience in a deep, transcendental way as we just pass them by in the street. The light of God is not a weird, supernatural awareness as other religions would suggest; rather it is something that can and should be seen in our works, in our lives. The light is meant to shine through what we do, through how we speak, through our attitudes, and through the way we relate to our fellow man, especially those who may not agree with or even like us.

Our lifestyles can open or close the door to people's hearts. When Jesus stands at their door and knocks, the testimony of our lives might well be the fact that leads a person to either open the door wide and let Him in, or close it and lock it with triple deadbolts.

This fact, more than anything, should bring us to our knees in the fear of the Lord, asking God to purify our lives and help us deal with whatever in our lifestyle is still not as holy as our heart is, through the blood of Jesus.

HYPOCRITE FOR JESUS?

Early in this book I shared how I rebelled against the traditional faith of my upbringing before encountering the reality of Jesus at age sixteen. About a year prior to my salvation, while still in my rebellion phase, a group of friends and I went on a party trip to Switzerland (which is *not* the same country as Sweden, by the way), where we booked ourselves into a hostel and planned to spend a few days partying.

One night as I was about to leave the hostel to go clubbing with my closest friends, I spotted a girl from our group sitting alone in the lobby. I didn't know her too well, but I noticed she was crying. Now, at that time of my life, I wasn't the kind of guy who would normally stop and intervene, but for some reason I felt bad at the thought of leaving her alone crying, so I told my friends to go on ahead and I would catch up with them in a bit.

I felt awkward approaching her since I barely knew her name and had no idea what was wrong. I asked if she was OK and hoped she would say, "Yes, I'll be just fine," so I could leave immediately with a good conscience. But she didn't. Instead, she started to cry even harder and shared with me how she had just found out her boyfriend had been cheating on her for the entire six months they had been together. Though she was only fifteen, they had been talking about getting engaged and then married one day, and she had thought he was the love of her life. After finding out he had been having sex with other girls all along, her life was shattered and she didn't know what to do. I sat there with no idea how to respond. Once I realized I had to say something, the only thing that came to mind was, ironically, the basics of Christianity that I had learned growing up.

So, feeling like the complete hypocrite I actually was, I told her, "God loves you, you know. If you pray, He will help you..."

She stared at me, her teary eyes now wide open.

"Joakim, are you religious? I had no idea!"

I felt even worse now! Here I was in Switzerland for one reason only—to run even further down the path of partying, clubbing, drinking, doing drugs, and getting as far away from God as possible. Yet I found myself encouraging this girl to pray to the same God I was busy running away from.

She started to ask all kinds of questions, and I tried to answer the best I could. Surprisingly, as we kept talking I realized that what I was saying actually made sense. I knew Christianity quite well in theory. And weirdly, the more we talked, the better I felt about sharing with her about God. Looking at this absurd situation in the rearview mirror now, I guess it was a seed of my future calling to preach that temporarily woke up from its deep sleep and thought, "Maybe there is hope after all!"

We talked for a good hour or more, and I could clearly see that what I said had a deep impact on her. Like many young people in Sweden, she had absolutely no idea about Christianity, no experience at all of church, and knew basically nothing about the Bible. But hearing the gospel for the first time, even though the communicator was only pretending to believe it, gave her hope and brought back that sparkle in her eyes. When I had finally run out of things to say, I told her I needed to go but that she should consider praying to God and trusting Him with her life and future. I stood up to leave, and when I reached the door I heard her call my name. I turned around and saw her smile at me.

"Joakim. Thank you so, so much!"

I went right back to feeling horrible again. Here I was, on my way out to partying hard and living like there was no God at all, and I had just convinced this girl that she should open her heart to the same God I was desperately running away from. How pathetic I was!

My conscience kept bothering me throughout that night, for good reasons, and I did not drink or do drugs with my friends. Because I was too much of a coward to let them know I was sober, I just pretended to get more and more plastered as the night went by.

At 2:00 or 3:00 a.m. we headed back to the hostel, screaming, shouting, and singing loudly—my friends because they were high, me because I was pretending to be. I took the lead as we arrived at the hostel, opened the front door, staggered inside, and let out a drunken bellow to try and act cool before my friends, showing them how drunk I was.

But as I looked up, there was the girl still sitting in the lobby, now staring at me. I could see the initial surprise in her eyes slowly turning to disappointment, then to disgust.

I didn't know what to do or say. I realized I had completely embarrassed myself and, way worse, that my lifestyle had just denied the message my words had shared with her. I was a fake, a phony, a hypocrite, and she knew it immediately. No one had told her about Christian behavior and lifestyle, but she knew instinctually that if I was the Christian I had professed to be earlier, I would not act this way.

She stood up, looked straight at me as tears again welled in her eyes, then turned around and walked to her room. I wanted to call her name, tell her I was sorry, but I realized there was nothing for me to say. She was right. Through my lifestyle I had just effectively locked the heart that was about to open up and had made it way less likely to ever open up again.

There is no happy ending to this story. I tried to approach the girl a few times throughout the remainder of the trip, but she never talked to me or even looked at me again. I have been praying that the shame I brought to the gospel would be forgotten and that God would again seek her heart. But all I know now is that I never want to make that mistake again. I never want to be guilty of allowing my bad example to damage or even destroy someone else's journey toward Jesus.

THE DAY OF VISITATION

In his first epistle Peter adds another important element to Jesus' command that we should let our light shine through good works, pointing toward God's love:

> Having your conduct honorable among the Gentiles,
> that when they speak against you as evildoers, they
> may, by your good works which they observe, glorify
> God in the day of visitation.
>
> —1 PETER 2:12, NKJV

Note the expression "in the day of visitation." This is written in singular, definite form—*the* day of visitation—suggesting that every person will, sooner or later, have this day, this moment, when God comes close and will provide them with their best opportunity ever to open their heart and say yes to His love and offer of salvation.

Now, the day you get to share the gospel or show the love of God through your lifestyle might or might not be the day of visitation for that specific person. But when that day comes—and only God knows when that is—all the seeds of the gospel and God's love that you helped to plant or water will come alive! This is why sharing the gospel and showing the love of God is never in vain, regardless of whether you get an immediate response or not. By showing someone God's love through your life, your attitudes, and your words, you invest in that person's upcoming day of visitation, making it more likely that when that day comes, he or she will open their heart and accept Christ.

Look back at your own story. I am quite sure you did not just say yes to Jesus and confess Him as your Lord the very first time you heard the gospel. Most likely, many small beams of the light of the gospel, of prayer, and of God's love shone into your life prior to that day, and then on your day of visitation it all came together, made sense, and helped lead you to the cross of Christ.

When you show kindness to someone, you flick the light switch of God's love.

When you don't respond in anger to the nasty comment on your Facebook, you flick the light switch of God's love.

When you choose to forgive and forget the hurt someone caused you, you flick the light switch of God's love.

When you offer to help someone in need and actually do it, you flick the light switch of God's love.

When you make sure your lifestyle communicates the same gospel your mouth claims to believe in, you flick the light switch of God's love.

And in doing so you are part of making sure that on the day of visitation, all these beams of light will come together to illuminate the path to salvation and redemption.

Maria, my amazing wife, heard a beautiful testimony a few years back emphasizing this very principle and reminding us how important it is to turn on the light by showing God's love.

Very much unlike myself, Maria gave her heart to Jesus at an early age and has spent her life serving Him since. She started leading worship at her church at age fourteen and was bold about sharing the gospel with her fellow students at school.

Many years later, when we had already met, fallen in love, and gotten married, Maria got an invitation to a fifteenth anniversary reunion of her graduation, where her former high school class would all get together to share memories over dinner. As she left our house on the night of the reunion, I remember how excited she was about seeing all her friends again. Later that same night I woke up to Maria shaking me violently: "Joakim! Wake up!" At first I thought the house was on fire, but then I realized it was just her being super excited about something that had happened that evening during the reunion.

She told me how, quite soon after the dinner began, one of her former classmates had come up to her and said she really needed to talk to her. This young woman had not been in Maria's closest circle of friends at high school, so initially Maria was a bit surprised. She knew about the girl, though, especially since after graduation she had become a famous recording artist in Sweden and had a number one hit song that every single person of our generation knew and could sing along to. Every time the song came on the radio, Maria always commented, "Oh! She went to school with me. We were in the same class!"

This young woman pulled Maria aside and said, "Maria, do you remember when you talked to me about Jesus?" Maria was completely taken off guard, but even though she tried to remember, she really didn't. The young woman reminded her of a seemingly insignificant moment outside a classroom when Maria had turned to her and said something simple about God loving her and how she could always call out the name of Jesus and He would listen. That was it. The conversation was so short that Maria couldn't even recall it, and the young woman said she had listened but had just shrugged it off. She wasn't a religious person at all and had no plans of becoming one.

Then the class graduated, and this girl had started singing in a band. An agent saw her perform, she was offered a record deal as a solo artist, and the rest was history. Her hit song had provided her with a celebrity lifestyle including all the fame and luxury she could possibly want and more. Then one day, many years after her big break, all alone in her luxury apartment, she had started to think about life and death, about the meaning of it all, about why she felt so empty even though she had everything money could buy.

"And then," she told Maria, "your words came back to me. For the first time in the fourteen years that had passed, I remembered the conversation we'd had word for word. And I remembered your example. I remembered looking at you at a distance and seeing someone who was really genuine, kind, and loving. It was like the memory of your words and the memory of your life blended together and convinced me: I need this. I need it more than my career, more than the money, more than the fame."

She told Maria how she had opened her heart and asked this Jesus to be her Lord. "And now," she said, shining with joy, "I am part of a church and have married a guy who is also a Christian. And I have just been so looking forward to seeing you again to say thank you!"

As we were sitting on our bed and Maria told me the story, we both had tears running down our faces as we once again were reminded that even the smallest initiatives, the tiniest prayers, the smallest acts of love that might seem so insignificant we don't even remember them, can actually change a person's life for eternity when that day of visitation arrives.

When we take initiatives of faith, when we pray, and when we show God's love, we are actually turning on the light in our world.

And again, when the light is turned on, God starts to work.

PART III

SHINE THE *Light*

You are the light of the world. A town built on a hill cannot be hidden. Neither do people light a lamp and put it under a bowl. Instead they put it on its stand, and it gives light to everyone in the house. In the same way, let your light shine before others, that they may see your good deeds and glorify your Father in heaven.

—Matthew 5:14–16

Chapter 11

SHINING THE LIGHT
OF THE GOSPEL

*W*HEN WE ALLOW the light of God to shine in and through us, we give God an initiative for Him to bless and use as a launch pad for His creative power to be released. Just as when you turn the light on in a dark room, the light will also bring clarity, revelation, and understanding. What was hidden in the dark is revealed in the light, what was vague and unclear is made visible and graspable, and the risk of stumbling and falling is way lower.

David writes, "In your light, we see light" (Ps. 36:9). In the light of God, shining out through us as the light of the world, the world around us can see God the way He really is. Not the image that religion, dead traditions, and lack of knowledge has created, but the real, true God in all His greatness, goodness, faithfulness, and love.

No one of us can reflect or light up every single facet of God's being and character—He is far too great—and that is exactly why He has created us distinctly, with different personalities and gifts, all displaying different aspects of Himself, and put us together to complete parts of one and the same body, the church. We are about to study more about all these different lights of ours in future chapters of this book. But for now, let's focus on some of the characteristics of our God that this world desperately needs to see. Specific lights have to shine throughout our worlds for God's kingdom to come and His will to be done.

THE GOSPEL LIGHT

The first one is the light of the gospel.

No calling given by Jesus to His disciples, then and now, has a stronger emphasis than the one to go into the world and share the gospel, the story of redemption through His name.

The Bible says that after Jesus' resurrection, He appeared to the disciples over a period of forty days and spoke about the kingdom of God (Acts 1:3). This is so amazing to me. A forty-day Bible school on the theme of God's kingdom, with a risen Christ as the teacher? Sign me up now! Still, hardly anything of this teaching is recorded apart from a few sentences. We can make no other conclusion than that these words by Christ are the summary of those forty days of post-resurrection teaching, the most important truths He wanted to communicate in those last few weeks with His disciples before being taken up to heaven. And when studying these sentences, they are all about the same two things:

- The call to share the gospel

- The promise of the help of the Holy Spirit

These two elements appear together at the end of all four Gospels and in the beginning of the Book of Acts. For clarity I have marked the callings to share the gospel with a (1) and the promises of God's help with a (2):

Matthew:

> Then Jesus came to them and said, "All authority in heaven and on earth has been given to me. Therefore go and make disciples of all nations (1), baptizing them in the name of the Father and of the Son and of the Holy Spirit, and teaching them to obey everything

I have commanded you. And surely I am with you always, to the very end of the age (2)."

—MATTHEW 28:18–20

Mark:

He said to them, "Go into all the world and preach the gospel to all creation (1). Whoever believes and is baptized will be saved, but whoever does not believe will be condemned. And these signs will accompany those who believe: In my name they will drive out demons; they will speak in new tongues; they will pick up snakes with their hands; and when they drink deadly poison, it will not hurt them at all; they will place their hands on sick people, and they will get well."

After the Lord Jesus had spoken to them, he was taken up into heaven and he sat at the right hand of God. Then the disciples went out and preached everywhere, and the Lord worked with them and confirmed his word by the signs that accompanied it (2).

—MARK 16:15–20

Luke:

He told them, "This is what is written: The Messiah will suffer and rise from the dead on the third day, and repentance for the forgiveness of sins will be preached in his name to all nations (1), beginning at Jerusalem. You are witnesses of these things. I am going to send you what my Father has promised; but stay in the city until you have been clothed with power from on high (2)."

—LUKE 24:46–49

John:

> Again Jesus said, "Peace be with you! As the Father
> has sent me, I am sending you (1)." And with that he
> breathed on them and said, "Receive the Holy Spirit" (2).
>
> —JOHN 21:21–22

Acts:

> But you will receive power when the Holy Spirit comes
> on you (2); and you will be my witnesses in Jerusalem,
> and in all Judea and Samaria, and to the ends of the
> earth (1).
>
> —ACTS 1:8

Five times—I repeat, *five* times—after the resurrection, Jesus establishes this clear theme, the summary of His teaching after the cross and the open grave: go and shine the light of the gospel, and as you do, God, the Holy Spirit, will be with you.

It is so profound, so clear, so simple, yet so often we have misunderstood this completely. The Holy Spirit has become something we speak of as an experience inside a church building rather than a helping presence in the process of sharing the gospel. When we speak about a "Holy Spirit revival," a "Spirit-filled church," or even the "presence of the Holy Spirit," we are hardly ever referring to shining the light, outreach, missions, evangelism, or sharing the gospel but rather to internal Christian experiences and events such as conferences, revivals, and church services.

Don't get me wrong. I love the local church and have been a pastor for almost forty years, and there are few things more precious to me than when the Spirit visits us in a tangible way and we experience His manifest presence as we gather in the name of Jesus.

But let us not forget that Jesus never talked about this being the main ministry of the Holy Spirit. The promise was not that the Father would send a Helper who would get us through life but one that would enable us to be witnesses for the gospel.

One of the greatest dangers for the modern-day church is that we become self-centered and start using, for our own pleasure and entertainment, the power God gave us so we could shine the light of the gospel. Then the church will become nothing more than a spiritual massage clinic for Christians rather than a battery charger enabling us to shine even brighter for Jesus.

May we never forget about the calling that was so central to Christ He repeated it no less than five times in between the resurrection and the ascension:

Go and shine the light of the gospel!

GIVING GOD AN INITIATIVE

Some years ago I shared this message about Jesus calling us to shine the light of the gospel and the promise of the Holy Spirit being connected to this commission. In the crowd at that time was a young man called Marcus, sixteen years old. He was challenged by the message, especially since like many Christians he never identified himself as someone that should, or even could, shine the light of the gospel and share Jesus with his world. But in that service he made a heart decision to take a step of faith, lift his staff, and turn on the light by giving God an initiative. He decided that come Monday morning he would open the door to his high school, walk straight up to whoever he saw first, and invite that person to his home group gathering that same night.

As Marcus approached the school building that Monday morning, he was shaking. But he remembered his decision and kept walking toward the school door.

Let me pause the story here for just one second. What

Marcus was going through at this time was truly a testament to the power of a decision. So many times we make wishes, form hopes, and express vague dreams, but they all tend to disappear, to dissolve into thin air, especially when pressure comes.

However, when we make a clear decision in the presence of God, a force is released inside us to see through whatever we decided. God Himself said about man: "nothing they plan to do will be impossible for them" (Gen. 11:6). This is said even about man's general capacity in himself, not even including his potential in God. The fact that you decide, or *plan to do*, something is of course not a guarantee it will in fact be done. The future process will still be up to our free will. But with a clear decision made in your heart rather than just a wish, you are much more likely to pull through and see what you dreamed in your heart become a reality before your eyes. This is one of the great purposes of the church: to lead us into the presence of God where hearts will open and decisions will be made that render us even more effective as we then go back into our worlds and shine the light.

WEIRDEST PARTY EVER

Back to Marcus. As he arrived at the school door, he said a prayer, took a deep breath, opened the door, and looked inside. The first person he saw was a guy his own age that he didn't know. Marcus initiated an awkward conversation, found out his name was Daniel, and eventually gathered the courage to invite him to the home group gathering that same night. However, Marcus left out one tiny detail: that it was a *Christian* home group meeting. Daniel was convinced he had just been invited to a party.

I later asked Daniel to write down the full story from his own perspective so I could retell it correctly rather than "evangelastically," and he sent me eleven pages of precise information. He described in detail how he got ready for the party that same afternoon, chose his outfit carefully, put on shoes that were good for dancing, used a cologne that he thought the girls would love, and headed out to the address Marcus had given him.

He found the house, rang the doorbell—and a mother opened the door. Daniel's mind went "Alert, alert! What's a mother doing at a house party?" Still confused, he was welcomed and led into the living room, where ten people were sitting around a table. One had a guitar. One had a tambourine. Daniel's mind was now racing. Who were these people? What in the world was this party all about?

He sat down slowly and suspiciously as one in the group welcomed everybody then said, "Let's start by singing!" Daniel was quite surprised at this, but he was singing in a choir and had a good tenor voice. Was this like a choir practice? Well, at least maybe he might impress the girls around the table by adding some nice harmonies.

The songs were all new to Daniel, but he tried to follow along from the lyric sheets available. Quite soon, however, he realized that all the songs were about God and Jesus. What was this? Why was it all religious? And why were some choir members singing with their eyes closed? Why were two of them lifting their hands in the air? Daniel had no past experience of church or Christianity and was really freaking out by now.

It got even worse. After the choir practice someone said, "Now let's pray." Daniel crossed his arms, thinking, "Oh no, I'm not doing that." He sat watching as the participants of the party started praying, one after the other. They were not reading preset prayers, as Daniel thought Christians did, but praying spontaneously, like talking to a friend. Daniel had never seen or heard anything like this and was quite fascinated but still totally convinced that he would not pray himself. No way!

But suddenly Daniel heard his own mouth speaking. Spontaneously, he said, "Could you please pray for my grandpa, who has been diagnosed with cancer and only has months left to live?" He was shocked at his own words. Why had he even said that? Why let these strange people into his private family issues? The group took him at his words, though, and prayed long and passionately for God to intervene in the situation.

After some ten minutes more of praying, followed by twenty of small talk, Daniel excused himself and walked home, thinking, "That was the weirdest party I've ever attended!"

However, one week later Daniel's mother called him while he was at school, ecstatic with joy.

"Daniel! They have taken new X-rays on Grandpa. The cancer that should have killed him within months is completely gone! The doctors don't understand anything. Daniel, this is incredible!"

Daniel's whole world stopped. Then he asked his mother exactly when they did the new X-rays. It turned out it was the day after the weird party he had attended.

Daniel called Marcus, saying, "Man, we need to talk." After meeting up with Marcus and talking about God a few times, Daniel came along with Marcus to my church, Word of Life. It was his first time inside a church, and there, up in the balcony, the presence of God embraced him. He cried as he got to experience God's love, and at the altar call he raised his hand and accepted Christ as His Lord and Savior.

Since then both Marcus and Daniel have attended our Bible school at Word of Life, and Marcus has served as a full-time missionary in China and Daniel as a full-time missionary in Thailand. Glory to God!

Yet none of this would have happened if Marcus had not made that initial decision to shine the light of the gospel.

Little did he know what he put in motion on that Monday morning by simply obeying the Great Commission for the first time.

Little do we know what God can do if we will only flick the light switch and shine the gospel of Jesus into our world.

Chapter 12

SHINING THE LIGHT OF MERCY

I LOVE THE PARABLES of Jesus. Not only their content and spiritual meaning but also the fact that Jesus just keeps telling stories to help us understand God and His kingdom. We were created by Him, and He knows exactly how our minds work—that we easily forget principles and points but remember stories. This is why I keep sharing testimonies in my teaching, as you know very well by now. The stories are not for entertainment or effect; rather, they are "the word becoming flesh," a way to make the spiritual principles graspable and applicable in our own lives by hearing and understanding how they were practiced in the lives of others.

Out of all the parables Christ shared, one of the most challenging, especially in this day and age, is the one about the unmerciful servant. Let's read it together:

> Therefore, the kingdom of heaven is like a king who wanted to settle accounts with his servants. As he began the settlement, a man who owed him ten thousand bags of gold was brought to him. Since he was not able to pay, the master ordered that he and his wife and his children and all that he had be sold to repay the debt.
>
> At this the servant fell on his knees before him. "Be patient with me," he begged, "and I will pay back everything." The servant's master took pity on him, canceled the debt and let him go. But when that servant went out, he found one of his fellow servants who owed him a hundred silver coins. He grabbed him

and began to choke him. "Pay back what you owe me!" he demanded. His fellow servant fell to his knees and begged him, "Be patient with me, and I will pay it back."

But he refused. Instead, he went off and had the man thrown into prison until he could pay the debt. When the other servants saw what had happened, they were outraged and went and told their master everything that had happened.

Then the master called the servant in. "You wicked servant," he said, "I canceled all that debt of yours because you begged me to. Shouldn't you have had mercy on your fellow servant just as I had on you?"

—MATTHEW 18:23–33

It is quite easy to understand the main point Jesus is trying to make: Because we have been forgiven, we should forgive. Because God showed us mercy, we should be merciful to our fellow man. However, we will not get the nuances nor the full understanding of the parable until we take a good look at the details.

The key is in the currency, you see.

THE KEY IS IN THE CURRENCY

In this story Jesus uses two specific sums of money for a very important reason, one that easily gets lost on us who live in a different time and can't relate to the value of money back then. So let's translate these amounts into something we can grasp and understand.

The first sum mentioned is the one the king's servant owed his master: "ten thousand bags of gold." The Greek word translated "bag of gold" is a very specific one, called *talanton*. A silver talanton equaled 6,000 denarii, which each represented an average day's wage. This meant that the silver talanton was equal to the amount of money one would make from having worked for about 16 years. However, Jesus specifies that these were not silver talantons but gold ones, which had a value of 30 times that of the silver version. This meant that one gold talanton, translated "bag of gold," would equal 180,000 denarii, or the wages from working every day for 493 years!

Even though this is already a crazy amount of money, Jesus doesn't stop there. The servant's debt to the king was not one but—hold on—ten thousand bags of gold, or gold talantons! This means a staggering 1.8 billion denarii, or about $295 billion. Makes you wonder how in the world the servant was able to spend all that. And it sure makes his argument before the king quite pathetic: "Just be patient, and I will pay it all back."

The point Jesus aims to make by using a sum of money His audience surely must have gasped at is obvious: every single one of us had a debt before God that we had no way of paying back:

> For all have sinned and fall short of the glory of God.
>   —ROMANS 3:23

Even by working hard for an entire lifetime, you would not see the debt decreasing at all. This was a problem we were unable to handle by ourselves, just as Isaiah prophesied: "all our righteous acts are like filthy rags" (Isa. 64:6).

And yet through Jesus, God would take the initiate to solve the problem on our behalf. Our debt was placed on Jesus, and He paid the full price for it so that you and I could go free just like the servant of the parable.

But as this man leaves the presence of the king, he bumps into a fellow servant who owes him money and refuses to show the same mercy that just released him from his mountain of debt.

Again, Jesus uses a very specific amount of money: the fellow servant owed the first servant "a hundred silver coins." The Greek word translated as silver coin is *denaria*, which we already stated means a sum equal to the standard salary for a day's work. Using the same math as before, a hundred silver coins would translate to roughly $16,000 in today's money.

We know Jesus used the first, astronomical sum of money to point out that we could never repay the debt we owe God. By using that amount, He was stating that we need a Savior, someone to pay the debt on our behalf. So what is the point He's trying to make by using this specific sum as the debt between the two servants? I mean, using a smaller amount of money—like one or two denarii—would have made the contrast between the two debts even greater.

I am convinced that Jesus uses the specific amount of a hundred silver coins for a distinct purpose. Sixteen thousand dollars is a significant sum. Having someone owe us this amount and finding out they cannot or will not pay us back would mean serious trouble for most of us. Losing that amount of money would create real problems, and you would definitely feel the pain of it.

So what Jesus is really saying is that, yes, a one-hundred-silver-coin debt *is* a lot. Maybe someone really hurt you, even abused you. Maybe you were seriously mistreated. Maybe someone betrayed you. Jesus is not denying, neglecting, or disregarding the pain you experienced from someone who wronged you.

However, $16,000 is only a significant amount as long as we don't compare it to $295 billion.

Jesus' message to us is simply this: remember the debt you had canceled. When we remember the enormity of what God has done for us, our gratitude to Him will grow immensely, and so will our eagerness to shine the light of mercy in our world—to people in need of the same mercy so that we, in turn, might help, support, and pray for them.

When speaking about shining the light of mercy and coming to the help of our fellow man in need, the name of one of my true heroes comes to mind. I hope her story and example bless and inspire you the same way they have me.

THE CHILD SMUGGLER

Irena Sendler was born on February 15, 1910, in Otwock, a town near Warsaw, Poland. As a young woman she pursued a career in social work and eventually joined the Warsaw Social Welfare Department as a trained nurse.

Growing up in a society with strong anti-Semitic currents, she saw firsthand the growing persecution of the Jewish people. But unlike most people of her day, Irena chose not to turn her head and hide behind the argument that this was not her problem. It was. It was her problem because she was a Christian who had been shown mercy by almighty God. How could she not pass on that mercy to her fellow man in need?

When World War II erupted in 1939, Poland faced brutal occupation by the German Nazis. Seeing the Jewish families now be subjected to even stronger persecution and discrimination, Irena felt compelled to act.

By this time the Jewish population of Warsaw had been gathered into a ghetto they were prohibited to leave. Historically, this and other Jewish ghettos turned out to be nothing more than waiting rooms for the upcoming concentration camps and the full-blown Holocaust that would lead to the execution of six millions Jews.

Irena realized the people inside the ghetto would eventually perish and that there would be no way to get them out of harm's way since the gates were strictly controlled by Nazi soldiers. But what about children? Maybe, just maybe, she could smuggle out some Jewish children from the ghetto.

Being a nurse, Irena volunteered to enter the ghetto on a daily basis and help out with basic health care. Even the Nazis saw the point of preventing epidemics that might spread out of the ghetto and become a problem for the general population of Warsaw.

Once inside the ghetto, Irena started secretly meeting with Jewish families, explaining the danger they were in and that she sadly would not be able to help them out of the ghetto nor save them from their upcoming fate. Still, she begged them to trust her with their children, and she promised she would do whatever she could to get them out of the ghetto and spare them a certain death.

Faced with this decision—among the most horrible any man or woman could make—many Jewish parents chose to trust her. They said tearful goodbyes to their own children and prayed they would make it out of the ghetto through the help of this young Polish woman and be saved from the fate of those left inside.

Irena had organized a network of courageous individuals who shared her commitment to help as many Jewish children as possible to get out of the Warsaw ghetto, and under the leadership of this young Christian nurse they used every means available to make that happen. When a dead body was brought out of the ghetto, they would place a Jewish child inside the body bag to be carried out alongside the corpse. Children were smuggled out through cracks in the ghetto wall. Irena and her team would even bribe craftsmen who worked daytimes inside the ghetto to smuggle Jewish babies out in their toolboxes at the end of the working day. Whatever it took, they were determined to get as many children out as possible, even though by doing so Irena and her friends were risking their lives every single day.

Once outside the ghetto, the rescued children were given new Polish names and forged identity papers and were then hidden in foster homes, orphanages, or convents. Irena wrote down the names of each child and its parents, along with all information needed to hopefully be able to reunite them after the war. Every night she placed notes for the new children rescued that day in a glass jar and buried it under a pear tree. Eventually the jar contained over twenty-five hundred notes, representing twenty-five hundred Jewish children that were saved from destruction.

In the last stages of the war, the Nazis finally discovered Irena's whereabouts, and she was arrested. Knowing there must be documentation of the children she had brought out of the ghetto, including where they could now be found and brought back, the Nazis tortured Irena to give up this information. Her arms and legs were broken, but she would not give up the location of the jar of notes. She was finally condemned to death, but her friends managed to bribe the death squad to release her on the way to execution, and she survived.

Irena always remained humble about her contributions, and it wasn't until many years later that her story gained wider recognition. In 1965 she was recognized as one of the Righteous Among the Nations by Yad Vashem, Israel's official memorial to the victims of the Holocaust. The international community gradually acknowledged her extraordinary deeds, and numerous honors and awards followed, including a nomination for the Nobel Peace Prize in 2007.

Irena Sendler passed away in 2008 at the age of ninety-eight, and I strongly encourage you to google images of her in her old age. She truly shines with joy! I look at her and think to myself, "That is the face of someone who did not live for her own comfort but to shine the light of mercy; someone who never hid behind excuses but, upon seeing the desperate needs of others, immediately asked herself what she could do to help."

Why? Because she realized she had been shown the same mercy herself by her own Creator and that the least she could do was pass it on to someone else in need.

Irena Sendler's life is such an inspiring testament to the transformative power of courage stemming from mercy. Her commitment to helping the needy, especially during the darkest days of the Holocaust, shows the profound impact that one individual—one light of the world—can have on the lives of others and on endless generations to come.

Let us always remember that since we have been mercifully released from a debt we had no way of paying back, the least we can do is look around us, asking who we can help, forgive, support, and strengthen in our turn.

Let us do whatever we can to shine the light of mercy!

Chapter 13

SHINING THE LIGHT OF TRUTH

*A*S WE NOW move on to another kind of light that is desperately needed in our world today—the light of truth—I want to start by sharing a story that rhymes well with the one about Irena Sendler from the previous chapter. This one too is set in the World War II era, and its main character is another one of my female heroes of faith: a largely unknown Christian girl who embodied the calling to shine the light of truth in her generation.

For most people the name Sophie Scholl doesn't ring a bell, but in Germany everyone knows about her. German TV named her "The Most Important German Woman of the 20th Century," and the nation's young generation voted her the greatest German who has ever lived. All this, even though she only lived to be twenty-one years old.

So who was this Sophie Scholl? If she were here to answer that question herself, she would probably say, "I am a Christian." But Sophie was not just any Christian; she was one who was convinced the Word of God can't just be heard. You have to live it, and you have to stand up for it even in times when you might have to stand alone.

Sophie Magdalena Scholl was born on May 9, 1921, in Forchtenberg, Germany, and was only twelve years old when the Nazis came to power in her homeland. To indoctrinate the young generation of Germany as early as possible to do anything for their leader, the German youth of Sophie's generation were recruited to Hitler-Jugend—Hitler Youth. Sophie joined when she was fourteen. Like all her friends, she got to march in uniform and was taught that she was an important part of her motherland and that her race was superior to all others. At first it was exciting. Sophie felt proud of being taken seriously and that the nation counted on her to give her life for something great, something noble. But as the days went by, something started to feel very wrong.

Sophie's father had raised her a Christian and taught her that all people are created in God's image—all are precious, and all are equal. And during Sophie's teenage years, she began to understand that what Hitler was saying was actually completely different from this. She was shocked when one of her Jewish friends was denied her basic human rights, and when Germany invaded Poland in 1939, Sophie realized that the message of the Nazi Party was the exact opposite of the message of the God she believed in.

In May 1942, at the age of twenty, Sophie moved to Munich to study at the Ludwig Maximilian University. By now she had seen so much injustice, hatred, and humiliation, especially toward the Jews, that she knew she had to do something. How could she even call herself a Christian if she would not stand up for Jesus and the truth in the midst of her nation's darkest hours? The Nazi reign of terror meant that raising your voice against Hitler equaled a certain death sentence—she knew that. But she was convinced she had to do whatever she possibly could for as long as she survived.

THE WHITE ROSE PAMPHLETS

Sophie and her brother Hans moved into a small student flat on Franz Joseph Street in Munich, and what happened there was nothing short of history. The two siblings and two of their friends formed the White Rose, a resistance group based on faith in Jesus, to wake the German people up and call for

resistance against Hitler. They bought a typewriter and an old
mimeograph machine and started writing pamphlets that they
copied by the thousands. These pamphlets were then secretly
mailed out to thousands of decision makers and influencers
across Germany. Sophie and her friends also secretly placed
stacks of the pamphlets in public spaces all over Munich,
including restaurants, schools, and restrooms, so that as many
as possible could grab a copy and read their message.

The six pamphlets of the White Rose are legendary examples of civil, Christian resistance against an ungodly govern-
ment. To quote some of the pamphlet essays of Sophie Scholl:

> Nothing is more dishonourable for a civilized people
> than to let itself be "governed" without resistance
> by an irresponsible clique of rulers devoted to dark
> instincts.

> Every word that comes from Hitler's mouth is a lie.
> When he says peace, he means war, and when he
> blasphemously uses the name of the Almighty, he
> means the power of evil, the fallen angel, Satan. His
> mouth is the foul-smelling maw of Hell, and his might
> is accursed at bottom.

> Since the conquest of Poland three hundred thousand
> Jews have been murdered in this country in the most
> bestial ways. Here we see the most terrifying crime
> against human dignity, a crime that is unparalleled in
> the entire history of mankind.

> If German people are already so corrupted and spiri-
> tually crushed that they do not raise a hand, frivolously
> trusting in a questionable faith in the lawful order of
> history; if they surrender man's highest principle, that

which raises him above all other God's creatures, his free will; if they abandon the determination to take decisive action and turn the wheel of history and thus subject it to their own rational decision; if they are so devoid of all individuality, have already gone so far along the road to turning into a spiritless and cowardly mass—then they clearly deserve their downfall.

Everywhere and at all times of greatest need, men have stood up, prophets and saints who cherished their freedom, who pointed to the One God and urged the people to a reversal of its downward course. Man is surely free, but without the true God he is defenceless against evil. He is like a rudderless ship, at the mercy of the storm, an infant without its mother, a cloud dissolving into thin air.

I ask you, you as a Christian struggling with the preservation of your greatest treasures, whether you hesitate, whether you incline toward intrigue or procrastination in the hope that someone else will take up arms in your defence? Has God not given you the strength, the courage to fight? We must attack evil where it is strongest, and it is strongest in the power of Hitler.

We will not be silent. We are your bad conscience. The White Rose will not leave you in peace![1]

The pamphlets of the White Rose spread like wildfire throughout Germany during the summer, fall, and winter of 1942. The Gestapo, Nazi Germany's secret police, was convinced they had come from a large national underground organization and worked like crazy to try to find and stop it. No one even imagined that these pamphlets, which influenced more and more people and helped them understand that Nazi messages went directly against God and His Word, really came from a handful of Christian university students.

Sophie and the other members of the White Rose knew from the start that it was only a matter of time before they were discovered, arrested, and executed. But they wanted to use the short time they had as well as possible.

On February 18, 1943, Sophie and Hans were walking the university corridors with bags full of their fifth pamphlet of protest against Hitler. With only minutes left before the bell rang, when classes would end and thousands of students would exit the lecture rooms, they placed stacks of the pamphlets outside every door so the students could grab a copy as they left.

When the bell sounded, Sophie was standing on the balcony of the university's main hall, overlooking thousands of students below her. She saw her own generation, now faced with the choice of either blindly following a diabolical leader even further into darkness or turning back to God and building a society based on love, peace, and equality. Sophie's heart was stirred, and she took the remaining pamphlets of the White Rose and threw them out over the students.

Surely she must have known, when she saw the pamphlets raining down over the students, that she would be discovered and caught. But I'm sure at that moment her own life and safety were the last things on her mind. If only she could help the young generation of Germany to wake up!

Sophie and Hans were immediately arrested, and the Nazis finally discovered that the White Rose, which had stirred fear throughout all of Nazi Germany, in fact only consisted of a few Christian students. Hitler wanted to get rid of this embarrassment as quickly as possible, and the day after the arrest, at a quick mock trial without any defense, the students were sentenced to execution.

As Sophie and her friends were led to the guillotine to be beheaded, she looked up at the clear sky and said, "Such a fine, sunny day, and I have to go. But what does my death matter, if through us, thousands of people are awakened and stirred to action?"[2] And the very last words of twenty-one-year-old Sophie Scholl, before her head was separated from her body, were, "God, You are my refuge into eternity."[3]

But as an unexpected final chapter in the story of Sophie Scholl and the White Rose, it turned out they had written a sixth pamphlet that they never got to print or distribute. This letter was smuggled out of Germany via Scandinavia to England, where it ended up in the hands of the Allied forces.

To honor the courage, determination, and selflessness of a German Christian girl named Sophie Scholl, the Allies made millions of copies of the White Rose's sixth pamphlet, loaded them into bomber aircrafts, flew over Germany, opened the hatches, and let Sophie's call to stand up for God and resist evil rain down from the heavens. The pamphlets that she herself saw rain down in the university auditorium now rained down for months over her entire country and her people!

Today, marble copies of the White Rose's pamphlets are embedded in the streets of Munich as a testament to the courage of a young Christian girl who lived her entire short life according to her motto: "Stand up for what you believe in, even if you are standing alone."[4]

WHEN TRUTH STUMBLES IN THE STREETS

After studying the life of Sophie Scholl, I believe her example is more important today than ever before. True, we no longer live under Nazi terror rule, and few of us will ever come close to paying the price she did for our convictions. But there are still truths under severe attack today. Truths that God assumes we will stand up for and defend.

Isaiah painted a picture of a people lost without God, one that sounds eerily similar to our society today:

> So justice is far from us, and righteousness does not reach us. We look for light, but all is darkness; for brightness, but we walk in deep shadows. Like the blind we grope along the wall, feeling our way like people without eyes. At midday we stumble as if it were twilight; among the strong, we are like the dead. We all growl like bears; we moan mournfully like doves. We look for justice, but find none; for deliverance, but it is far away.
>
> For our offenses are many in your sight, and our sins testify against us. Our offenses are ever with us, and we acknowledge our iniquities: rebellion and treachery against the Lord, turning our backs on our God, inciting revolt and oppression, uttering lies our hearts have conceived. So justice is driven back, and righteousness stands at a distance; truth has stumbled in the streets, honesty cannot enter. Truth is nowhere to be found, and whoever shuns evil becomes a prey.
>
> —ISAIAH 59:9–15

The prophecy then moves on to describe the Lord's reaction to this:

> The LORD looked and was displeased that there was no justice. He saw that there was no one, he was appalled that there was no one to intervene; so his

> own arm achieved salvation for him, and his own righ-
> teousness sustained him.
>
> —ISAIAH 59:15–16

It is so fascinating to me that as the Lord looks down on fallen humanity, as He sees righteousness stand at a distance and truth stumble in the streets, His first reaction is to look for someone to intervene, to stand up for truth, and then being *appalled*—the Hebrew word really means "shocked"—because no one does. God rightly assumes that whoever calls Him Lord will see it as their duty to support truth when it stumbles, to stand up for righteousness when it is under attack.

When that initial plan failed and no one was prepared to shine the light of truth in their generation, God intervened Himself—not because this was His main plan; it obviously wasn't. His first choice, as we have learned by now, was to have someone take an initiative, raise a staff, shine a light, and then He would start working. But since His people were not doing what they should and had run away from their responsibilities, God had no other option than to overrule them and go to work Himself. But He was "shocked" by having to do so.

Let us make sure God doesn't have to be shocked at our indifference or lack of commitment to stand for truth in our generation.

Too many times we see truth stumble and react only by whining, complaining, and posting horrified posts on Facebook. God demands more from us than that.

He calls us, His church, "the pillar and foundation of the truth" (1 Tim. 3:15). If the church compromises with the truth, the pillar and foundation of society will crumble. If we fail to speak out against evil and injustice; if we fail to speak out for the defenseless, the unborn, the poor, the defenseless; if we fail to come to the rescue of truth, freedom, and righteousness in our world, we will leave God horrified and this world broken.

Never forget in what spirit we should shine the light of truth. There is no room for judgmentalism, pride, or a holier-than-thou mentality in the kingdom of God. Shining the light of truth is not about waging war on people. It is about placing yourself in the gap between God and a fallen world and interceding from that place. What God was looking for in Isaiah 59 was someone who would "intervene." The Hebrew word literally means "standing in between, standing in the gap."

Again, our greatest example is Jesus Himself, who the Bible says was "full of grace and truth" (John 1:14). Jesus was uncompromising about the truth yet managed to communicate it, live it, and shine it in such a way that sinners were not pushed away but rather attracted by Him. Why? Because the truth He shone was steeped in grace. His purpose was not to judge, confront, or prove Himself to be better than them but to love them and point the way back to the Father's house.

That is what the light of truth is all about—the light that this world so desperately needs today.

Chapter 14

SHINING THE LIGHT
OF COMPASSION

*F*OLLOW ME" (MATT. 4:19).

Two simple words, and the two men listening threw away their nets, their source of comfort and income, to obey and follow.

What we sometimes miss here is that this was not actually the first time these two men had met Jesus. Sometimes we think it was, which makes the story incredibly strange. Like, how could they do such a thing? Why would they leave everything behind to follow a complete stranger who just happened to come by the beach and say two words?

But it wasn't some magic in the words of Christ that made them follow Him that day. It had nothing to do with some special aura, a shining halo above His head, or magic dust left in His footprints. They already knew Jesus. They had been close to Him ever since the day in the Jordan Valley in Judea when their former master, John the Baptist, pointed to Christ and encouraged them to follow Him instead (John 1:35–42).

So the two simple words spoken to these young men by the Sea of Galilee were not their first invitation to follow. It was a challenge to take another, new step together with Him. To not just know, or know about, Jesus but to actively follow Him wherever He was going, and in the process become fishers of men.

So how does that relate to you and me today? Well, if Jesus is the same yesterday, today, and forever (Heb. 13:8), then I believe He says the same things to His disciples yesterday, today, and forever. If He said "follow Me" to His followers back then, He is saying "follow Me" to His followers today, to you and me.

We are often very quick to respond, "Yes, I will follow You! I want to go where You are going!" We confess it, we pray it, we sing it in our songs, and rightfully so. Obviously this is the right response. But before we so wholeheartedly answer the call, there is a question we should ask ourselves that we many times forget about:

Where is He going?

Honestly, the first thing you would want to know before making a holy promise to follow someone is where that person is heading. Because if you are really serious about going with them, you will end up where that person ends up. His or her final destination will become yours.

THAT WHICH IS LOST

Back in 1987 I promised to stay by my wife's side for the rest of my life. But before I gave her that promise and she gave me hers, we had gotten to know each other and spent hours and hours talking and praying. We had seen each other's lifestyles and talked about visions, priorities, dreams, and plans for the future, and we had both come to the conclusion that, yes, I want to be with this person forever. I want to follow along with this person, because he/she is heading in the same direction I want to go, toward a destination where I want to end up.

So where is Jesus going? Where will your destination be if you are serious about wanting to follow Him?

There is one very clear answer to that question, because Jesus has been very open with us regarding His destination. He is heading toward a specific goal that He explains in Luke 15, where He gives us three special parables: the lost sheep, the lost coin, and the prodigal son.

The interesting thing is that these three parables all make the exact same point, which is unusual for the teaching of Jesus. Normally He would illustrate one spiritual truth using one parable, then move on. In a few cases He uses two stories to emphasize the same point, but only in Luke 15 does He use three parables to underline the exact same truth. We cannot interpret this any other way than that whatever Jesus wants to communicate here is really, really important.

In the first parable we are introduced to a shepherd who leaves ninety-nine sheep behind to look for the one that was lost. I praise God that this was not a Swedish shepherd—who probably would have thought to himself, "Oh well, I still have ninety-nine left. There's always some amount of loss; no worries." But this shepherd had a different mindset, a different heart. He just could not accept the fact that a sheep that belonged to Him and ought to be safe in His hands was now lost. So He left His entire flock behind and went looking for that which was lost until He found it.

In the next story we encounter a woman who lights a lamp in search of a lost coin, refusing to be satisfied with the nine already in her possession. Her joy when she finds it is so great that she throws a huge party for the whole neighborhood. (We looked at this parable in chapter 6, remember—stating that you and I are the "lamp" of the story?)

The last of the three parables is the well-known story about the prodigal who asks for his inheritance before due time and leaves to spend it on a sinful lifestyle. Eventually he comes to his senses and decides to return home, where his father restores him and gives him so much love and attention that his older brother, who has been at home the whole time, gets jealous.

As far as content, these three stories are completely different. But their theme is exactly the same. In each of the parables you will find:

- something that is in the right place
- something that is in the wrong place
- a person representing Jesus

Now ask yourself this question: In these parables, what is it that grabs Jesus' full attention? Is He busy focusing on what is in the right place or that which is in the wrong place? I think you see an interesting pattern. The shepherd, the woman, and the father—all representing Jesus—turn their full attention to that which is in the wrong place, that which is lost!

And if we still for some reason miss the point Jesus is trying to make, even though it is emphasized in three different parables, one after the other, He makes it clear one more time just a few chapters later: "For the Son of Man came to seek and to save the lost" (Luke 19:10).

With that in mind, let us go back to the main question. Do you remember it? "Where is Jesus going? Where will I end up if I am serious about following Him?"

The answer is that Jesus is heading in the same direction He always has been. He is going to find the lost sheep. He is going to find the lost coin. He is going to welcome back a lost son or daughter. He is going to those who need Him the most. He is going to all those He has died for but who may never have had an honest chance to hear about Him and say their own personal yes to Him.

On the way to that which is lost, that which is in the wrong place, He turns around, looks into your eyes, and says: "Follow me." Not just to church on Sunday but to find the lost sheep, the lost coins, and the lost sons and daughters of your world and reality. And from the bottom of His heart, He hopes that you will still say yes to the call, like generations before you.

THE PRICE OF FOLLOWING

There is a clear price tag to this following of Jesus. It means putting the welfare of the lost sheep, coin, and son or daughter before your own. It means sacrificing your own comfort, your own resources, sometimes even your dreams and ambitions, to help someone else see the light. In our self-centered and individualistic age, this might look like a high price to pay, a heavy cross to carry. But the truth is, nothing this world can offer you will even come close to the satisfaction of knowing you are really following Jesus. And step-by-step His heart will take form in yours, His passions will become yours, and the divine compassion that made Him choose the pain of the cross over the glory of heaven will become your driving force.

I want to share another story with you, and this one is very special to me. As you might have noticed by now, I love history and using true stories as examples to emphasize spiritual truths. But without a doubt this story is the one that has made the deepest impression on me personally. I pray it will touch your heart the way it has touched mine.

"OTHERS!"

On May 28, 1914, at 4:30 p.m., the ocean liner *Empress of Ireland* left the harbor in Quebec, Canada, and started its journey to Liverpool, England, manned by a crew of 420 and carrying 1,057 passengers.

With less than two years having passed since *Titanic*'s voyage across the Atlantic ended in tragedy, most of the passengers on board the *Empress* would surely have had this terrible event fresh in their minds as they boarded the ship. However, the thought of the same thing happening once again—that another ship's journey would end in hundreds of lives coming to an end—must have seemed impossible to them.

But, sadly, what seemed unbelievable was about to happen. In the early morning hours of May 29, the *Empress of Ireland* collided with a Norwegian coal transport ship called *Storstad* in the thick fog of the mouth of the St. Lawrence River. The collision ripped a huge hole in the hull of the *Empress*. The actual impact felt quite mild; survivors later said they didn't even notice anything had happened until the sirens started to sound, but the damage was devastating. The *Empress* was rapidly taking on water through a hole of over 300 square feet, and the entire ship disappeared into the dark water just fourteen minutes after impact. Few people even had the chance to react before it was too late, and when the tragic event was over, 1,027 out of the 1,477 people on board had lost their lives. Unlike *Titanic*, which stayed afloat for hours after the impact, enabling many passengers to be saved through its lifeboats, there had been no time to launch even one of the lifeboats of the *Empress*. Your only chance of survival in the freezing cold water was if you had gotten hold of a life vest that would keep you afloat until help arrived. And very few such life vests had been available.

For some reason the *Empress of Ireland* tragedy would fade from history, and today few people have even heard about it. Still, its tragedy would contain a hidden story of Christian heroism, incredible self-sacrifice, and the ultimate consequences of following Christ to save those lost.

This story gradually unfolded as the testimonies of the survivors were compiled and one after the other shared the same strange experience. They kept referring to people who were later identified as being part of the same group—a young group of passengers from Canada's Salvation Army who, under the lead of thirty-five-year-old Edward James Hanagan, were on their way over to England to take part in a large Christian conference.

Several survivors shared how they had made it out of their cabins but had not been able to get a life vest before they ended up in the ice-cold water. They had quickly realized they would not have the strength to stay afloat for long and that it would only be a matter of minutes before they sank beneath the surface and met the same fate as so many others on this terrible night.

But then they had seen someone swimming toward them—a young person who fought their way through the freezing water, and when coming close enough, had taken off their own life vest and thrown it to them. Essentially giving up their own life for someone else.

One of the most heart-wrenching of all these similar stories came from a grown man who had ended up in the water, but since he could not swim, he realized that his life would be over in a few minutes. Then suddenly he had spotted a young girl, maybe eighteen or nineteen years old, swimming toward him. He saw how she struggled against the waves and currents and finally managed to come close enough to throw her own life vest, her only chance of survival, to him. The man caught it, but despite his wish to survive, he felt he could not keep it and watch the girl perish. She was just a young girl, only half his age. So he threw the life jacket back to her and called out for her to save her own life instead.

This made the girl furious. She threw the vest back to him and shouted a few short words that he would never forget: "Take it! I will die better than you tonight!"

All these young people who unselfishly and spontaneously

reacted in the same exact way were later identified as being part of the Salvation Army group.

When I first heard this amazing story, I asked myself: What was it that caused this group of young Christians to instinctively put others before themselves? What was it that caused them all to think "I must save someone else" instead of "I must save myself"?

It surely had to do with the nature of Christianity that their leader had taught them. General William Booth had died, or been "promoted to glory," as they so wonderfully put it in the Salvation Army, just two years earlier, but his teaching and perspective on following Jesus had made a huge impact on his whole movement.

General Booth had seen an incredible growth since he founded the Salvation Army. At the time of his death in 1912, the movement had already been established in over fifty countries. Each year the general would send a telegram with instructions to all his workers across the world, casting vision about where the organization was headed and what to focus on in the near future. But during the last few years of his life, his telegrams had become shorter and shorter.

The last telegram he ever sent contained just one word— one that summarized the whole movement and its focus, and also the foundational direction for the entire Christian life:

"Others!"

What he was actually telling his movement was, "If you focus on others, everything else will work out. If you focus on others, God will take care of you too. If you focus on others, you'll have the right perspective on your life and what following Jesus is all about."

That word and the lifestyle of compassion were what motivated the young people on that cold night in May 1914 to sacrifice their own lives if it meant saving a lost sheep, a lost coin, a lost son or daughter. And I have a feeling that the word *others* needs to be written on the hearts of Christians again today, in capital letters and with a permanent marker.

In an age that is more selfish than ever, there is a need for a new generation of Christians who will head in a different direction.

One that will be motivated by compassion for the lost rather than their own gain and comfortability.

One whose gut reaction will not be "What's in it for me?" but "How can I help someone else?"

One that is willing to follow Jesus all the way to His final destination, to shine the light of compassion and illuminate the path that leads all the way home.

PART IV

YOUR *Light* IS UNIQUE

I praise you because I am fearfully and wonderfully made; your works are wonderful, I know that full well. My frame was not hidden from you when I was made in the secret place, when I was woven together in the depths of the earth. Your eyes saw my unformed body; all the days ordained for me were written in your book before one of them came to be.

—PSALM 139:14–16

Chapter 15

YOU ARE AN ORIGINAL

S O WE HAVE discovered together that God is light, Jesus came to reignite the light that went out, and He now entrusts you with the very same task He had when He walked the earth: to be the light of the world; to take an initiative, pray, and show God's love—and thus flick a spiritual light switch on so that God's power can be released into the world.

Now it's time to deal with what inspired me to share this message and write this book in the first place: the fact that too many Christians think they are unable to let their lights shine and make a difference for God in their reality.

Most of the time the problem lies not in theory nor in theology. Most Christians know that Jesus calls them the light of the world in the Gospel of Matthew, and they have probably heard a message or two about it but still lack the confidence and boldness to put that calling into practice. Why?

As a pastor for almost four decades, and especially after having worked with young people for most of that time, I know from experience that much of the problem stems from a belief that only a certain kind of person—an ideal Christian with a distinct personality—has the ability to shine for God. It is so easy for us to paint a picture in our mind of this "super Christian" person with no faults and challenges, elevated high above the rest of us. And if you don't recognize yourself in that perfect image you've created in your mind, it is also easy to assume that "shining the light" is not for you. You assume that you lack whatever is needed and subconsciously disqualify yourself from even the remote possibility that you could actually be the person who flicks the light switch and makes a difference for Jesus.

Oh, how I wish there were a button I could push to instantly and supernaturally set you free from this devastating lie! If we would only see the truth—that *all* of us are created to shine, that *all* of us have the ability in Christ to do so, and that *all* of us have been entrusted with a unique flavor of light that only we can shine in our unique world—then the church would be turned into a Jesus revolution, the gospel would sweep the earth, and the kingdom of God would flourish.

In the absence of such a magic button, let us try to deconstruct this lie and remind ourselves of the truth of God's Word. In doing so, there are three important things to understand:

1. Shining your light does not require perfection.

If it did, none of us would be able to shine at all. It is a lie of the enemy and a complete misconception of the message of the Bible that God demands perfection before He can use anyone for His kingdom. According to the Word of God, the reality seems to be quite the opposite way around.

> Brothers and sisters, think of what you were when you were called. Not many of you were wise by human standards; not many were influential; not many were of noble birth. But God chose the foolish things of the world to shame the wise; God chose the weak things of the world to shame the strong. God chose the lowly things of this world and the despised things—and the things that are not—to nullify the things that are, so that no one may boast before him.
>
> —1 CORINTHIANS 1:26–29

When the light of God reappeared on earth through Jesus Christ, it passed by the perfectionists. The wise, the religious, the ones who considered themselves worthy of God through the way they kept the commandments of the Law, were left behind and many times became enemies of the light. Instead, Jesus chose regular, ordinary people and gave them the mission of shining for Him. The people He proclaimed to be the light of the world in the Sermon on the Mount were not theological students or participants of a pastors' conference but fishermen, carpenters, tax collectors, former prostitutes—the kind of people no one counted on or expected anything good from.

This was all according to the wisdom of God. If the light were to shine through the perfection, wisdom, and strength of man, then man would get the glory. But if it shone through the foolish, the weak, and the unexpected, then God and God alone would be glorified.

This is exactly why it is so destructive to believe we have to reach a point of perfection before we are qualified to take an initiative and trust God to use us. The outcome of this will only be that we wait in vain for a level of excellence we will never reach while the world around us is left in darkness.

Remember, throughout the Bible God continuously used men and women who were far from perfect, people with major flaws in their lives such as Abraham, Tamar, Moses, Samson, David, Solomon, Jonah, Elijah, Jeremiah, Peter, James, and John. Does this mean our lifestyle doesn't matter and that we can just keep on sinning and still expect to be used by God? Of course not. The Bible clearly tells us to stop sinning (Rom. 6:12), to work out our salvation in the fear of the Lord (Phil. 2:12), and not to gratify the desires of the flesh (Rom. 13:14). There is absolutely no place in Christianity for a teaching that implies we can do whatever we want, or that God's grace means I am automatically forgiven anytime I sin.

The point is that even though God requires holiness and expects us to continuously strive so that our heart's salvation also works its way into our minds, habits, attitudes, words, and deeds, He will not stand at the sideline and wait for a certain level of perfection before He can use you.

He wants to shine through you right here and now!

2. You were created to shine a unique light.

You are not in this world and in this time by coincidence. Quite the opposite. God did not just design you to be the person you are, He also designed the time and place where you would live your life. Your personality, your year of birth, and the part of the world in which you were born—all are parts of God's master plan.

> Praise be to the God and Father of our Lord Jesus Christ, who has blessed us in the heavenly realms with every spiritual blessing in Christ. For he chose us in him before the creation of the world to be holy and blameless in his sight. In love he predestined us for adoption to sonship through Jesus Christ, in accordance with his pleasure and will—to the praise of his glorious grace, which he has freely given us in the One he loves.
>
> —EPHESIANS 1:3–6

Please read that again and again until you fully realize how amazing this perspective is. He chose you not just when you were born or even conceived in your mother's womb. He chose you before the creation of the world! Before that first "Let there be light" He thought of you and planned you. You were already designed in God's heart before He even designed creation, and He chose you to shine before the first man drew his first breath.

God knew what He did when He gave you your unique personality and the ability to shine your unique light in your unique world in your unique time. This is the reason you are not like others and should never compare yourself with others. Why should you, when you are perfectly put together by God almighty, entrusted and enabled to shine exactly the light needed for the people around you to see.

Comparing yourself with others (only to fall short in the process) is one of the most common and devastating mistakes Christians make. Now, there is a positive kind of comparison, where we can look at other people's faith, initiatives, and examples and be inspired to reach even further ourselves. But placing yourself next to someone else, only to assume that because you are not like them you are less able to shine and less likely to be used by God, basically means claiming that God has made a horrible mistake.

You are you—created and chosen by God to live in this world and in this time to shine a light uniquely designed by the Lord Himself to reach the exact group of people God knew from the beginning your life would touch.

3. Diversity is not a problem but an asset.

In the world we live in conformity is the law. Everybody is expected to look the same, be the same, act the same, have the same opinions, and wear the same clothes. Standing out from the crowd or going against the flow is punished by cancellation. In a season of insecurity, when you are desperately seeking identity, the easiest route is simply to be a clone of everyone else.

As Christians we can never allow ourselves to be infected by this mindset. In the kingdom of God diversity is not a problem but an absolute necessity. No one of us can display the fullness of God on our own. No single person, church, or movement carries in itself the ability to reflect to the world the greatness and diversity that is found in Him. He is simply too great, too amazing.

This is exactly why we, as the church, are portrayed and described as one body with many different parts rather than as many independent individuals:

137

> Just as a body, though one, has many parts, but all
> its many parts form one body, so it is with Christ. For
> we were all baptized by one Spirit so as to form one
> body—whether Jews or Gentiles, slave or free—and
> we were all given the one Spirit to drink. Even so the
> body is not made up of one part but of many.
>
> Now if the foot should say, "Because I am not a hand,
> I do not belong to the body," it would not for that reason
> stop being part of the body. And if the ear should say,
> "Because I am not an eye, I do not belong to the body,"
> it would not for that reason stop being part of the body.
> If the whole body were an eye, where would the sense of
> hearing be? If the whole body were an ear, where would
> the sense of smell be? But in fact God has placed the
> parts in the body, every one of them, just as he wanted
> them to be. If they were all one part, where would the
> body be? As it is, there are many parts, but one body.
> The eye cannot say to the hand, "I don't need you!" And
> the head cannot say to the feet, "I don't need you!"...
>
> Now you are the body of Christ, and each one of
> you is a part of it.
>
> —1 CORINTHIANS 12:12–21, 27

How I love this revelation! And how totally contrary it is
to the way of this world, which dictates that everyone should
be the same. The kingdom of God is the complete opposite, a
kingdom where diversity is celebrated as absolutely essential.

We are called to complete, not to compete. And as we all
shine our individual, unique lights in our individual, unique
worlds, all of them will blend together into one amazing beam
of light for the world to see. The result: one and the same light
but filled with all the various spectrums and nuances needed
to display the greatness, glory, and diversity of our God.

This has always been the main vision, passion, and desire

of my ministry: inspiring believers to shine their lights boldly in their world and never excuse or exclude themselves because their lights don't look exactly like someone else's.

An Illustrated Sermon

Some years ago, after many months of prayer, God gave me the grace to put together an illustrated sermon for this very purpose. By that same grace, this message has now encouraged hundreds of thousands of believers in some fifteen countries to shine their lights, and that same sermon is also the source of inspiration for this book.

The main illustration of the message consists of a number of lampstands with different light bulbs—all different in design, but all with the ability to shine their unique light according to the purpose they were created for. As the light bulbs light up one by one, I talk about each one, its importance, its strengths and limitations, and how its uniqueness sets it apart from the others and gives it a very special purpose that none of the others can fill. Then at the end the lamps all light up at once and their unique lights blend together to create this beautiful display of unity and diversity—just as the kingdom of God is meant to do.

As I now introduce you to these different light bulbs to help you better understand the diversity of the kingdom and the uniqueness of every believer's light, maybe you will be able to identify what kind of light bulb God has created you to be and why your special light is so important and irreplaceable. Of course, these are not all the light bulbs in the kingdom, nor does every one of us necessarily relate to just one of them— most of us may well be a combination of many.

It is my hope and prayer that your heart will be encouraged and that the light bulb illustration will help you avoid one of the greatest traps of Christians: believing the lie that our unique personality is a problem rather than a potential in God's eyes.

Chapter 16

THE APRICOT SOFT LIGHT BULB

*T*HIS LIGHT BULB was the one that gave me the idea for this entire illustration, and it has remained the first example in line ever since.

Many years ago I was at a hardware store looking for a light bulb to replace a broken one in our kitchen. As I looked through the regular bulbs, trying to find one with the right base, wattage, and tone, I saw a box that looked very different. It said "Apricot Soft Light Bulb" and contained one bulb that was apricot/orange in color and matte-finished. I was curious about what it would look like shining and put the bulb in one of the department's empty sockets.

Once turned on, the bulb spread this warm and cozy apricot-colored light all around. Compared to the other clear-daylight bulbs next to it, its light was less intense and in-your-face but added this nice element of warmth and comfort. It gave a relaxing, homey atmosphere, one you would really appreciate when you came home at night after a long, hard day of work.

As I stood there looking at the apricot soft light, I started thinking about Jesus calling us to be the light of the world and that even though we are all called to shine and able to shine, our lights are slightly different, adding various aspects of God's own nature. And I thought, "We sure need those apricot soft light bulbs in our churches!"

Maybe you are just that kind of light bulb in the hand of God. Maybe He has given you that soft, comfy light to shine to help people relax and open up their hearts for the Holy Spirit. Maybe one of your main gifts is all about turning churches into

141

families as you help create an atmosphere that makes people feel at home and at ease—that they belong and are truly loved.

My wife, Maria, is a big-time apricot soft light bulb. She is the kind of person who, if left in an empty, bare room for five minutes, will somehow have it stocked with couches, rugs, curtains, soft lights, scented candles, and someone playing the violin in a corner! When our family is having coffee together, which happens most days, Maria always sets the table as if it were someone's birthday and takes such delight in making sure everything is as beautiful and nice smelling as possible—just to put a smile on all our faces.

In our church we try to make sure to have our apricot soft light bulbs design and decorate the premises, as well as welcoming new visitors and following up those who have made decisions. I always love seeing how that special, inviting light they spread is melting down the walls and encouraging hearts to open up.

If you are one of God's apricot soft light bulbs, let me tell you this: We need you in God's kingdom! We need you in the church! And this world desperately needs to see that unique light of yours as it shines for the glory of God.

"APRICOTS" SHINING THEIR LIGHT

Early in this book I told you about the refugee influx to Sweden back in 2016 and 2017 and how our church chose to intervene. Though this humanitarian disaster caused a huge social challenge for my country through the immigration of tens of thousands of people in a very short time, God challenged us to keep a perspective of faith, daring us to believe that inside this complex situation there would be seeds of opportunities and revival.

This was not without its challenges. The scenario of the

refugees fleeing the Middle East, escaping ISIS, emerged extremely fast and left us only weeks before this stream of people arrived in Sweden, worn out after first traveling the Mediterranean Sea in inflatable boats and then walking across Europe, carrying their children.

To bring full focus to this urgent need and the potential inside it, we had to put the emergency brake on most of our regular programs and activities. All staff, regardless of department, became involved, and hundreds of church members volunteered to meet these urgent needs and do whatever they could to shine God's light in the middle of the refugees' darkest night of fear and uncertainty.

I will never forget what I saw during those first weeks and months of the refugees arriving: how the lights from an army of apricot soft light bulbs were turned on and started to shine their comforting light into the dark desperation of all these men, women, and children from the Middle East.

We put a huge banner on our church showing the words "Refugees Welcome" with a big red heart. Every day our members came to church bringing food, clothes, and toys by the thousands, and we worked night and day to distribute it all to the newly arrived families. The doctors and nurses of our church were involved in providing free medical care to the refugees. We organized bus rides from the temporary refugee camps to our church, our young people arranged classes in the Swedish language for the refugees, and our business men and women gave classes in how to start up a business in Sweden to make sure the people were integrated into society rather than left on the outskirts of it, supported by governmental funding only.

Our whole church life orbited around this situation. We had refugees sleeping in our auditorium until they were provided with temporary housing, and many church members opened their own homes and had families of refugees stay with them for months.

Most of these activities, initiatives, and new programs were not organized by the church alone but by our members seeing needs and stepping up to meet them, and in doing so they allowed the comforting apricot light of God's genuine love to shine into hearts that had never experienced it before.

The Muslim refugees kept asking us, "Why are you doing this? Why do you love us? If it were you coming as refugees to the Middle East, we would not treat you this way!"

And we kept telling them: the symbol of our faith is not two arms crossed, saying no, but two arms wide open to form the shape of a cross, ready to receive and love anyone who comes our way.

As the warm, inviting, and non-confrontational apricot soft light kept shining all over our church and into the drained hearts of the refugees, we saw God move in a powerful way— as He always does when the light comes on—and the Muslims open their hearts and accept Christ by the hundreds. It became the rule rather than the exception that a few days after we shared the gospel of Jesus with a Muslim individual or family, Jesus would appear to them in a dream or open vision to confirm what we had told them was true. They were getting healed from sicknesses and diseases, having life-changing encounters with Christ, and wanting to get baptized by the hundreds.

Still today, years later, the vast majority of those getting saved and baptized in my local church are men and women from the Middle East—many of them former Muslims—who have come to faith in Jesus Christ. We never expected to have so many church members called Mohammed!

We even had to start a special Bible school for former Muslims, and over the past few years we have graduated more than 450 students from it.

Today I look back with such a grateful heart at this amazing and completely unexpected development, how all these people that were out of reach for the gospel while in their home countries were suddenly brought within the reach of Jesus. I tremble at the thought of how easily we could have lost this opportunity simply by taking another approach and not stepping out of our comfort zone as a church.

And I thank God, more than anything, for the mobilization of the apricot soft light bulbs in our church, who could shine a light so warm, so attractive, and so welcoming that even those we never thought would even approach our church were attracted to it and therefore heard the gospel and gave their hearts to Jesus.

Thank You, God, for all the apricot soft light bulbs of the kingdom!

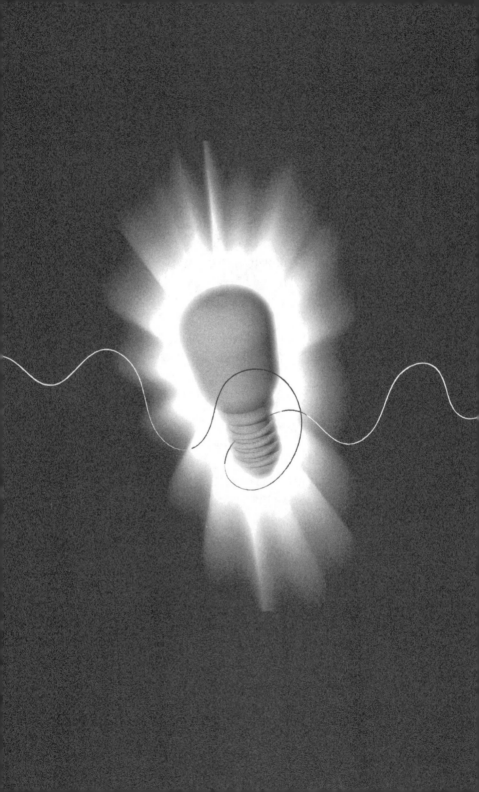

Chapter 17

THE OVEN LIGHT BULB

*T*HE NEXT LIGHT bulb we are going to look at is one of my genuine favorites: the oven light bulb.

Now, oven light bulbs are not seen as much as the other ones. They normally stick to their oven and keep away from attention. The oven light bulb does not have that urgent need to be seen and heard, nor to be the center of attention all the time. It is a bit of an introvert and is more than happy not to be publicly acknowledged for letting you know when the cheese on your frozen pizza is deliciously golden brown. The oven light bulb knows its thing, sticks to it, and does a great job.

Since the oven light bulb is a bit smaller than the other light bulbs and does not claim a whole lot of space, sometimes it might feel as though it is not as important as the rest of them. But let me tell you about one ability this light bulb has that everyone else lacks: the oven light bulb can take the heat of 500 degrees and still keep shining!

When the pressure builds, the temperature climbs, and other light bulbs pop from the heat, the oven light bulb keeps serving, keeps shining, and keeps holding its ground.

It might not be as flamboyant as some of the others, but the oven light bulb is faithful, passionate, hardworking, loyal, and fully committed to standing its ground. And it would be impossible to build the kingdom of God on this earth without all the millions of oven light bulbs we are blessed to have among us!

I believe that on the final day of judgment, after our working day on earth is done, many will be surprised by how many unknown oven light bulbs will hear the words "Well done, good and faithful servant! You have been faithful with a few things; I will put you in charge of many things. Come and share your master's happiness!" (Matt. 25:21). The greatest crowns handed out on that day might not go to the light bulbs who were seen more than the rest but to those who were faithful in the small things and kept silently serving, kept shining for God, even in high temperatures.

WHEN NOTHING MAKES SENSE

In Judges 20 we find a story that is a bit peculiar but in the end very encouraging and a great testament to the oven light bulb mentality.

The backstory is that eleven of the tribes of Israel had declared war against the twelfth, the tribe of Benjamin, because a group of men from this tribe had committed a terrible crime and raped a woman to death in the city of Gibeah. Her family demanded that the men be delivered and held responsible, but the tribe of Benjamin instead chose to protect the criminals. This led to the rest of Israel declaring war on them to ensure that justice was done according to the Law of Moses.

When you think of it, this looked like a done deal. Many stories in the Bible, with David and Goliath as the classic example, tell us how the good guys were a minority but with God's help ended up victorious. But this time the good guys actually outnumbered the bad by far. Israel's army counted four hundred thousand warriors while Benjamin had just twenty-six thousand in their army (vv. 14–17).

In addition to their huge numbers, Israel also knew they had a righteous cause. Their aim was that the criminals be punished and justice administered according to God's Word. They even sought God for guidance for the battle and received it (v. 18). How could anything possibly go wrong?

But the inexplicable happened. When Israel's army proudly marched into a battle that should have been a piece of cake for them, they encountered a catastrophic defeat. Twenty-two thousand of their soldiers were killed in the battle, and Benjamin hardly lost any.

There must have been a lot of questions in their minds when they returned to their camp, but they chose to knock the dust off themselves and get back up on their feet. They asked God if they should once again go to war against Benjamin, and God confirmed, "Go up against them" (v. 23).

All right then. Maybe they misunderstood the first time. It seemed that for some strange reason something went wrong, but this time it would all be fine.

The army gathered new courage, their banners again lifted high, swords gleaming in the sunshine, and victory back in their eyes—but they were defeated a second time. Another eighteen thousand soldiers perished in the battle.

Confusion. Chaos. What on earth had happened? The camp was now speechless, bewildered, but still came back into the presence of God. There they wept together, fasted, prayed, sacrificed, and asked for a third time: "Shall we go up again?" The answer came from the Lord: "Go, for tomorrow I will give them into your hands" (vv. 26–28).

And finally, the next day Israel won a rightful, enormous victory over Benjamin. But when we read about it, we are not really jumping around, cheering and shouting. The only thing we want to know is what happened the first two times. Why were they defeated when they should have won? Why did they meet with failure even though everything was on their side, even God?

If only the author of Judges had offered seven reasons for the defeat, seven things we can learn from it, and seven principles for not having it happen again. But the Bible does not give us a single answer or explanation.

The reason I even bring up this slightly confusing story is because there are times in our lives when this exact thing happens. When we do the right thing. When we are honest and have pure motives. When we have the promises from God. But still things do not turn out as planned and hoped for. What do you do then?

This story might not give us explanations and reasons for why things happened the way they did, but it does give us some valuable lessons on how to handle these situations.

Stay close to God.

Even though Israel did not understand what had happened, they didn't turn away from God. Yes, they wept, and it's OK to weep. Yes, they mourned and asked why, and it's OK to do so, even though at times you may have to accept that you might never get a good answer.

The thing that really catches my attention is that they "wept before the LORD" (v. 23). Many people distance themselves from God when inexplicable things happen. Some even blame Him. Don't do that. It is when your world is shaking that you need Him more than ever.

Without Jesus we lose perspective, but when you stick close to Him and maybe even cry a bit on His shoulder, you will soon hear His voice saying, "I am with you. Go up again."

The oven light bulbs know better than to run away from God when tough times come. They will run right to Him!

Don't lose courage.

This can be easier said than done sometimes, I know. But Christianity is not a spa or a holiday retreat. Your faith can be costly at times, and you and I are far from the only people in church history who have had to take the big with the small.

God has never guaranteed an easy ride, but what He has promised is that every adversity you face will have passed through a filter that is adjusted to your ability. "And God is faithful; he will not let you be tempted beyond what you can bear. But when you are tempted, he will also provide a way out so that you can endure it" (1 Cor. 10:13).

When something goes wrong in your life, do a quick checkup and see if there is something you might have done wrong, something you should have done differently, or something you can learn for the next time. If you don't find anything like that, leave the burden in the hands of Jesus and move on. As you do, seek advice, help, and prayer from your brothers and sisters, pastors, or others God has placed there so they can be by your side. No one of us is called to do life on our own.

Keep shining!

"Should we go up against them again?" What an amazing attitude from a group of people that had just suffered two inexplicable defeats. Here they were, all showing the characteristics and chanting the life mottoes of oven light bulbs: "Don't give up! Go on! Try again! Keep shining even in the heat of the hour!"

We are living in the age of fast results, but the fact is that many doors will not be opened just because you bang on them once. You need to back off, get ready, and bang again in the same place. And again. And again. For how long? Until the door opens.

A lot of times the breakthrough is the closest when the resistance is the greatest. Right at that point, all it takes is for us not to give up. Will we get battered at times? Yes. Will we sometimes feel a bit confused and wonder why? Yes. Will we sometimes feel like "Man, it would be so nice to just give up now"? Yes.

But in spite of this, the oven light bulbs of God teach us to faithfully continue to shine, in fair wind and headwind, for better and for worse, because inside they know that if they just don't give up, sooner or later there will be victory. Sooner or later the breakthrough will come.

Thank You, God, for the oven light bulbs of the kingdom!

Chapter 18

THE CRYSTAL LIGHT BULB

*T*HE NEXT LIGHT bulb I want us to look at is one that really helps us see the diversity of the kingdom and which adds a tremendous blessing to it when allowed: the crystal light bulb.

The crystal light bulb is one made for the chandeliers of the halls of power. It is designed to shine its light in rooms of influence, where big decisions are made. These light bulbs are those within the body of Christ who are called to be business-people, politicians, decision makers, journalists, influencers— those designed to either generate resources and momentum for God's kingdom or serve its purposes and values by using their influence to promote truth, justice, and righteousness while pointing people to Jesus.

And oh, how we need to see an army of bright, shining crystal light bulbs in our world today.

If you are one of them, you've probably known it for some time—and so have your parents. They probably told each other "this one is a bit special" ever since you started a student union in kindergarten or became the Judge Judy of your class, negotiating with the principal about longer recess!

Or perhaps that crystal light bulb calling was stirred later in life, when you saw the example of someone else making an impact for Christ outside the classic church ministry setting. Their example helped you realize that being used by God did not necessarily require becoming a pastor or evangelist. Rather, "whatever you do, do it all for the glory of God" (1 Cor. 10:31).

A lot of times crystal light bulbs are given way too little focus and space within Christianity, and the body of Christ has suffered for it. I remember reading Hobby Lobby founder David Green's biography in which he shares about his painful wrestling with God's call to go into business rather than full-time church ministry as all his brothers and sisters did, and how unspiritual and backslidden he initially felt by becoming a businessman. Unfortunately, this is a struggle shared by way too many crystal light bulbs, who have been left feeling less spiritual just because the light they've been given by God is not mainly designed to shine within the four walls of the church (though they desperately need the church to be able to shine bright outside of it).

It's time for us to recognize and encourage all the crystal light bulbs of the kingdom, pray for them, and give them all the support they need. The kingdom will not expand in our societies by excellent messages being preached inside its church buildings but through light bulbs being lit outside of them. And maybe the greatest reason for a message to be preached in the first place is to encourage and inspire just that.

Throughout history, the crystal light bulbs of the kingdom have initiated some of the most radical and important societal changes this world has ever seen. One of these changes was brought about by a man who received his own crystal light bulb calling at the tender age of fifteen.

ABOLISHING THE SLAVE TRADE

In the year 1774, a British teenager named William was listening with fascination to a preacher who shared his dramatic testimony with a church crowd—and the story was definitely worth hearing.

The preacher, whose name was John Newton, told about how he used to be the captain of a ship transporting slaves to the colonies of the British Empire. He told of how he had been responsible for the kidnapping of thousands of Africans and transporting them under terrible conditions to the new nations where they would be sold as slaves into lives of misery and darkness.

But then he shared how, during a violent storm, he had looked death in the eye and realized he feared it more than anything. Thus he had cried out to God for salvation. As he did, the storm immediately calmed down and the sinful captain surrendered his life to Christ, receiving forgiveness for his sins. Newton went on to write the hymn "Amazing Grace" based on his own testimony and dedicated the rest of his life to two things: preaching the gospel of Jesus and doing whatever he could to fight the slave trade.

The young man listened, almost breathless. His heart lit up with God's light, and right there and then young William decided what his life would be all about from that moment on. As long as he had another day left on earth, he would live it to fight the evil of slavery in the name of Jesus and for the glory of God. He would give his entire life to the cause of erasing this moral darkness from his homeland and its empire.

William did not lose any time. Yes, he was only fifteen years old, but he nonetheless realized that if he were to influence society in the way he now dreamed of, it would not be enough to preach in a church pulpit. He had to gain access to the influencers and decision makers of his time. Somehow he had to get inside Parliament.

So William studied intensively (when you see a fifteen-year-old boy study hard, you know God is up to something), and just a few years later, at age twenty, he reached his first goal as he was elected into the British Parliament as its youngest member ever.

Once there he launched phase two of his plan: he started to prepare an inflammatory speech against the slave trade. He researched, wrote, and went over the arguments time and time again until everything was watertight and perfect. It would take him ten full years of preparation before he was satisfied and ready to hold his life's speech at the British Parliament.

In the year 1789 the day had finally come. Trembling, but sensing the sweet smell of victory, William entered the pulpit of the Parliament to hold his speech, titled "The Abolition of the Slave Trade." After delivering the three-and-a-half-hour speech, he requested a vote to declare slave transportation illegal within the British Empire. But William was defeated by a broad majority. Many of the members of Parliament owned slaves themselves and were not very keen on losing them.

But William was not the kind of crystal light bulb to give up at first resistance. He went back to his office and refined his speech to make it even better, even more effective. One year later he was back in the Parliament pulpit. Same speech but a little better. A new vote! And a new defeat. Back again next year. Defeated. Back again the year after that. Defeated again.

Each year William bounced back. Five years of annual speeches and votes passed. Eight. Twelve. Fifteen. William's annual failure was becoming a tradition, and it would take eighteen years before the final breakthrough came and his bill to criminalize the transportation of slaves was finally passed by the leaders of the British Parliament.

Victory, but still no time to waste. Now it was time for William to enter phase three of his life strategy: to make sure that every existing slave within the Empire became a free woman or man, in the name of Jesus.

This final project took an additional twenty-four years of hard political work, fighting major resistance. But in March 1833, William—now seventy-four years old—finally got to see the fulfillment of his life's dream. Parliament eventually voted for his proposition, making slavery illegal throughout Britain and its colonies. That day, almost one million people became free men and women.

Only four days after the historic vote, this crystal light bulb was turned off for the very last time. William Wilberforce went to be with the God of light forever, and as he entered heaven, I am certain the first words he heard were, "Well done, good and faithful servant" (Matt. 25:21).

If your calling in life is to be a crystal light bulb, live that calling! Shine your light! Run with the vision God has given you! Because let me tell you: this world needs you, and the body of Christ is not complete without you.

Thank You, God, for the crystal light bulbs of the kingdom!

Chapter 19

THE PARTY LAMP

*T*HE NEXT LAMP I want to talk about is a very special one. It might be frowned upon by some, but how very boring things would be without the party lamps of the kingdom.

This is the personality that adds energy and volume to everything and shines with a pulsating, multicolored, disco ball kind of light. The party lamps will find any reason to celebrate and always carry a smoke machine around, just in case. At night they can be seen cruising downtown in bright yellow Ford Mustangs, seemingly only powered by their state-of-the-art speakers throbbing at full volume. The steering wheel has nothing to do with steering—it's a volume control!

And they always fall asleep at Bible study...

The party lamps of the kingdom remind us that attraction precedes evangelism—that to be effective at communicating the gospel, we must catch people's attention first. The party lamps suffer pain from hearing boring Christian messages from the pulpit, seeing low-quality Christian websites that have not been updated in seven years, or viewing so-called Christian social media posts more focused on judging the world than saving it. They don't suffer for themselves; they do so at seeing how the greatest message in the world is packaged and presented.

Oftentimes the party lamps' input and effort to bring constructive criticism is shrugged off by the other lamps, who may claim that the party lamp is too "worldly" in its mindset and perspective. And it doesn't help that the party lamps are not really known for their diplomatic skills but instead can come across as quite direct as they speak their minds, making the other light bulbs even more defensive.

But how beautiful things would be if we learned to listen to the party lamps once in a while, allowed them their place in the kingdom, and encouraged them to shine their special light.

Sure, every single lamp has its own set of advantages as well as risks, and yes, God's party lamps must realize that not everything about the church is high energy and maximum volume. But the rest of us also have to realize that we need the party lamps in order to not fall asleep or die from boredom.

I love the party lamps of the kingdom. I love their energy, their passion, and their constant focus on celebrating, spreading joy, and making sure everyone is having a good time. Also, many times when the light is turned on inside a party lamp through faith in Jesus, an amazing evangelist is born.

"ASK ME WHY!"

Some years ago a sixteen-year-old guy called Johan gave his heart to Jesus at a summer youth camp in Sweden. Invited by a friend, Johan had no prior Christian experience and was not raised by a Christian family. This thing about Jesus was completely new to him. And one of the first messages he ever heard in his brand-new walk with God was me sharing that he was called to be a light in the world, and when he turned on the light through an initiative, God's power would be released.

Johan made up his mind right away. When he got back to high school after summer break, he would sure turn the light on in his world! And being a definite party lamp—hair dyed bright yellow—he would make sure this light would be seen by everybody.

Johan started by taking a photo of himself in a cool "gangsta" pose. Then he made a poster out of the photo, adding the words "I am a Christian. Ask me why!" He made fifty copies of the poster and put it up. All. Over. His. School. Wherever the students now looked throughout the halls and rooms of the high school, Johan the Party Lamp was looking right at them, encouraging them to ask him about the reason why he had become a Christian.

Only two days later Johan called me (I still don't know how he got my number, but party lamps always seem to find a way) and was overjoyed. He said, "Pastor, this was the best thing I have ever done! In two days only, over forty students have come up to me, pulled me aside, and asked me why I have become a Christian! And I got to share Jesus with them all!"

I was so amazed and so happy hearing this. You see, because Sweden is one of the most secularized nations in the world, many wrongly assume that people are simply not interested in God. Yet nothing could be further from the truth! Surveys among Swedish teenagers show that a vast majority of them are interested in questions about faith and religion. So the challenge is not that people are not interested; the challenge is that they don't know where to go with their questions.

For most Swedes, it would be completely unnatural to google "churches nearby" since they have never been to a church and don't know what happens there. So the real answer to the problem is making sure that as many light bulbs of God as possible are lit up in their own world. Then, and only then, will we see how hungry for God this world really is!

Johan, who had only been a Christian for weeks, found himself sharing Jesus, praying for people to come to know the Lord, discipling his own group of new converts, and bringing them along to his church.

We shared the amazing testimony of Johan's poster with all the young people in the New Generation school movement, and soon these posters were put up in schools all over Europe in all kinds of languages: *"Je suis chrétien, demande-moi pourquoi,"* *"Soy cristiano, pregúntame por qué',"* *"Jeg er en kristen, spør meg hvorfor."* One single party lamp idea had inspired tens of thousands to shine their light openly and publicly!

AN ARMY OF PRAYING OLD LADIES

Hungry for more, and with the endless energy found in party lamps of God, Johan got ready for the next level of shining. He had heard me talk about how prayer turns the light on and started to pray for his school himself, but he wanted support. He had not been a Christian for long but had already heard about the church phenomenon called "praying old ladies." For some reason, it seemed every church had a group of them, and they really knew how to pray from a lifetime of experience.

So Johan the Party Lamp called the pastors of all the local churches in the area, asking for the names and phone numbers of any praying old lady they had in the church. Once he had collected a long list of names and numbers, he called the praying old ladies one by one, politely asking them to pray for revival in his school during one specific hour every week. Soon Johan had every school hour of the week covered by his newly mobilized army of praying old ladies.

He also asked the old ladies to pray for a new strategy of his. Johan had the idea that if the most notorious bully, the toughest guy in school, were to get saved, that would echo throughout the students and make a genuine impact. The guy Johan had in mind—we'll call him Ahmed—was a Muslim and did not seem at all interested in changing his religion, but would he be able to resist the strategic prayers of the old lady army? Johan did not think so.

Said and done, the ladies started praying for their assigned hour every week and for Ahmed to be miraculously saved. A few weeks later Johan was in a class that was just over, busy packing his books and getting ready to leave the room, when he looked up and realized the only ones left in the lecture hall were him—and Ahmed.

Johan's heart started pounding. He had never personally talked to Ahmed, and for good reason: this guy was known to beat people up even unprovoked, and most just tried to stay as far away from him as possible. Still, Johan now painfully perceived that he had become his own answer to prayer. He took a deep breath, stumbled across the room to Ahmed, and stuttered that he had something to tell him. Then he shared the gospel of Jesus as fast as he possibly could, thinking he might well be lying unconscious on the ground at any moment.

But Ahmed listened to every word. When Johan was done, and a bit out of breath, Ahmed said to him: "Interesting. These past few days I have been thinking about God and faith. I've been a Muslim all my life, but recently I have felt that something is missing. And for the first time I have asked myself if I might be connected to the wrong god? And then here you come and tell me about Jesus."

Johan slowly realized the whole setting had been perfectly planned by God and that the prayers of the old ladies had had maximum effect, preparing this heart to open up as Jesus knocked. As the two teenage boys left the classroom together a bit later, both were sons of God, both had Jesus as their Lord, and both were filled with the Holy Spirit. And according to Johan's strategy, the rumor spread and led to many more students giving their hearts to Jesus.

This beautiful story reminds us again that nothing is impossible for God when someone flicks the light switch. It also shows us some of the amazing things that can happen when the infectious light of a party lamp is turned on.

Thank You, God, for the party lamps of the kingdom!

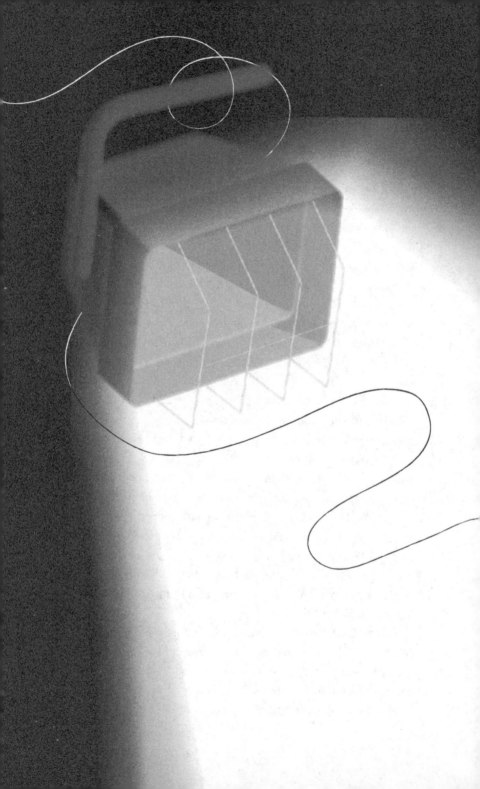

Chapter 20

THE WORK LIGHT

*L*ET US INTRODUCE another important member of God's great family of lamps and light bulbs: the work light.

What makes this one stand out is the intensity of its light, which is extremely bright and almost impossible to look at directly. This lamp is not in the game of creating a pleasant, enjoyable atmosphere but—as the name suggests—is there to work. Its light exposes dust and dirt that would escape the light of most other lamps and light bulbs. Rather than the light of a beautiful sunset, this one is more akin to the painful rays of sunlight that pierced your teenaged eyes as your mother violently pulled the curtains of your bedroom after you had slept in until 2:00 p.m.

I sometimes refer to this lamp as the "prophetic" lamp since its personality carries many resemblances to the prophetic ministry seen in the Old and New Testaments. The work light is motivated by a strong zeal for God and holiness. It can smell sin at a mile's distance, and its bright, piercing light will expose it, point it out, and call for repentance. Nothings stays in the dark when the work light is around!

The work light is the kind of person who starts most sentences with "Thus saith the Lord" and is likely to have Handel's "Messiah" oratorio playing on repeat in the car. This person might be reading the Bible through three times a year and is a little frustrated by the fact that all the other lamps aren't. And by the way, they don't like the party lamps at all—there is just no place for such worldly lamps in the kingdom of a holy God!

The work lights of the kingdom are there to remind us that following Christ is not a game or a part-time hobby. When the church has been too influenced by the world, their light might feel painful on the eye, but many times it is just what is needed to wake us up and call us back to the cross of Jesus once more. The work lights are always there for prayer meetings and always ready to share a word of God.

Like all lamps and light bulbs, the work light personality has its pros and cons. Due to its high standards, the work light can sometimes come across as judgmental and might fall short of patience and grace. A classic New Testament example of work lights is found in Luke 9:

> As the time approached for him to be taken up to heaven, Jesus resolutely set out for Jerusalem. And he sent messengers on ahead, who went into a Samaritan village to get things ready for him; but the people there did not welcome him, because he was heading for Jerusalem. When the disciples James and John saw this, they asked, "Lord, do you want us to call fire down from heaven to destroy them?" But Jesus turned and rebuked them.
>
> —LUKE 9:51–55

The first thing we need to realize when we read these verses is that Jesus loved John and James. These two disciples were among the three closest to Him out of all the Twelve, and this incident did not change that. Jesus knew they were speaking out of the zeal of their hearts and their fear of God when they suggested calling down fire on a Samaritan village. But they channeled their zeal in the wrong way, which is also a classic challenge of the work lamp.

The Word says that Jesus was "full of grace and truth" (John 1:14). These two elements, both facets of God's nature, did not oppose each other in the life of Jesus. Instead the one completed the other. To the woman caught in adultery (John 8:11), Jesus said: "Neither do I condemn you," which is grace, followed by, "Go now and leave your life of sin," which is truth.

So though the work lights normally have all they need in their kingdom "truth tanks," they sometimes need to refuel their "grace and love tanks" and stop suggesting that fire be called down on those who don't meet their standards.

ANGELS, HORSES, CANDLES...AND A WEBSITE

A few years ago I had an unusual encounter with an unexpected work light.

I had just preached the final service at our annual youth conference at Word of Life. Hundreds of teenagers had responded to the altar call, and we closed the service in a great atmosphere of afterglow in the Holy Spirit.

A long line of young people wanted to meet me afterward to say hi, and in the corner of my eye I saw this young guy, maybe sixteen years old, seemingly waiting until I was done talking to all the others. Finally he came up to me and told me, with a very serious face, that he had a problem and needed to talk to me in private. Once we had moved over to a corner of the church and sat down, he shared what was bothering him. He opened by saying, "I come from a very prophetic church."

Already I felt uncomfortable. Don't get me wrong—I love prophecy and the presence of the Lord, I believe in the gifts of the Spirit, and at our church we always give room and time for God to move in any way He wants. But there was just something about how this young guy talked and acted that told my heart something was wrong here. He kept going:

"And a few months ago one of our leaders had a prophetic vision over me. He saw one candle that was lit on my right side, and one that was not lit on my left. Then he saw an angel on my left side, but no angel on my right. And then he saw horses galloping above my head."

I couldn't believe my ears.

"I don't understand this vision. And I feel that until I get the interpretation of it, I will be at a plateau in my spiritual growth."

By now I just felt sorry for him.

In my heart I asked, "What have we done to Christianity? Why do I sit next to a sixteen-year-old boy who should be out there living a fresh, joyful, inspiring life with God but is instead trapped in this completely absurd so-called prophetic vision? 'A plateau in my spiritual growth'? What sixteen-year-old even uses that vocabulary?"

He continued. "And tonight, as I heard you speak, God told me that you have the divine interpretation of this vision."

His last sentence caught me completely by surprise. Oh, so I was now supposed to provide the interpretation of the weirdest "vision" I had ever heard of? What in the world could I say that would make any sense in the introspective Christian world that this teenager was caught in? What could I do to encourage him to enter the beautiful, exciting reality of a life focused on helping others and sharing Jesus?

I thought for a while and prayed silently in my heart. Then I had an idea. It was a bit wild, but I trusted that it was from the Lord. I turned to the young man and said, "I have the interpretation! The vision means that God wants you to share the gospel of Jesus with somebody."

He looked very surprised and seemed quite disappointed that the vision did not have a fancier interpretation. He immediately responded by saying that he couldn't do that and didn't know how. So I asked around to find out about his interests and passions. He answered that he normally spent almost all his time on his computer—which explained a lot.

So I told him, "OK, then go and build a website about Jesus. Nothing weird or fancy, just the basic John 3:16 gospel of Christ, and share the site with everyone you know."

For the first time since we met, I saw a small sparkle of light in his eyes.

"You know what? I could actually do that!" he said.

So we prayed, he left, and I quickly forgot about him until, a few weeks later, he sent me an email full of capital letters and exclamation marks. He told me he had built the website, shared it with everyone he knew, and already had thousands of visitors. He had added an email address that could be used for any questions about Jesus or Christianity, and now he triumphantly shared with me that he was answering people's questions on faith all the time!

In my heart I really hoped those answers would not include candles and horses, but throughout the email it was obvious there had been a shift of balance in this young man's life—one that is so important for us all and especially for the work lights of the church: to never grow so "spiritual" or church-oriented that we distance ourselves from the Great Commission.

I could not help but reply to his email by asking, "What about the angels, the candles, and the horses?"

Within a minute, a one-line reply came back: "I've forgotten about those!"

Which to me, honestly, was the greatest news ever. You see, the light of God shining through you may be unique, but it should never alienate you from the world you are called to reach.

But having said all this about the need for balance and perspective in our lives—we are so blessed to have the work lights among us to keep us on our toes, to help us remember that we serve a holy God, and to inspire us to reach even higher.

Thank You, God, for the work lights of the kingdom!

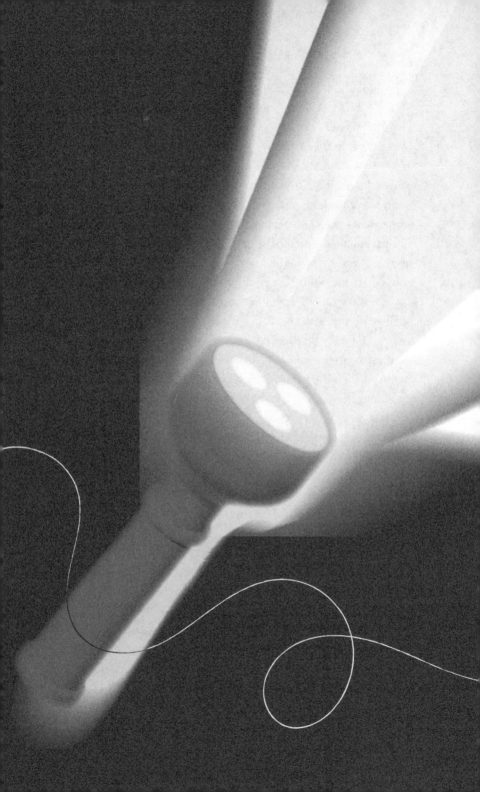

Chapter 21

THE FLASHLIGHT

*T*HE NEXT LAMP I want to present in this diverse family of "lights of the world" within the kingdom of God is the flashlight.

What makes this lamp so unique and important is that unlike the other lamps and light bulbs mentioned, the flashlight is cordless. It does not have to be attached to a certain output. Or city. Or nation. This is why it can go out into the whole world and shine the light of Jesus. The flashlight is truly the missionary lamp of God!

If you are one of these lamps, you might well have been wired a bit differently from the start. You might have found yourself passionate about traveling, seeing new cultures, meeting new people, and discovering that the world is so much bigger than your own present perspective.

It is very encouraging to me that so many young people these days want to travel and see the world. I believe that God has placed the seed of a missionary, the flashlight identity, in more people than ever from this generation. Many might not yet have connected with God through faith in Jesus and therefore don't yet realize that what they might consider a passion or general interest is in fact God's future call upon their lives. Yet God chose them before the foundation of the world and knitted them together in their mother's womb, providing them with a personality and passions that are a perfect match to their calling. Seeing so many young people passionate about traveling, I interpret it as God mobilizing an army of missionaries to go out into the world and bring in the final harvest before Christ's return!

THE FLASHLIGHT CALLING

It's important to point out that whichever lamp you may be, every one of us shares part of the flashlight calling and needs to step into it. The Great Commission, to "go out and make disciples of all nations, baptizing them in the name of the Father and of the Son and of the Holy Spirit, and teaching them to obey everything I have commanded you" (Matt. 28:19–20), includes every single one of us. Still, there are some that carry the call to be a lifetime flashlight and perhaps move from one reality to another to fulfill that special calling.

Back in the mid 1980s, God gave a special word to our church. He challenged us to raise forty million Swedish krona (about four million US dollars) in four years and invest it in preaching the gospel in what would soon be the former Soviet Union. At the time our church consisted of about five hundred people, and they had just given generously to the building of a new church auditorium. But I praise God that our church is a mission-minded one! Our people came together, passionate to reach the Russian people, who had been starving spiritually during seventy years of Communism. As we started to raise the funds together, we didn't really see how we would be able to invest them in missions inside this nation, which at that time was completely closed to the gospel of Jesus.

But God knows times and seasons! Exactly when we, by God's grace, reached the goal of forty million krona (and then some), the walls of the Soviet Union fell like a house of cards, the chain of Communism broke, the nation opened up—and we were armed and ready!

Our first step was to buy hundreds of video cassette players (anyone remember?) and send them all over Russia. Then we recorded hours and hours of teaching of the Word of God, dubbed into Russian, onto videotapes that were distributed all over the nation. Russians—starving for the truth, for freedom, for Jesus—gathered all over the massive nation to watch, accept Christ, and grow in their faith.

A GOSPEL WHISTLESTOP TOUR

Quite soon after our gospel invasion into Russia started, we came across a former KGB (secret police) officer who had overseen spreading the communistic propaganda throughout the Soviet Union under its former leadership. He did not share our faith but was inspired by our passion and offered us a train that had been used to spread the Communist propaganda throughout the former USSR. For two years in a row we sent teams of young people from our church that loaded this train with New Testaments and Bible teaching books in Russian, then traveled up and down the continent to spread the good news about Jesus.

In every city on the route, the teams stopped, did street evangelism, handed out books, prayed for people on the streets, and saw people come to faith in Christ en masse. When the train passed smaller villages, it slowed down, and the teams opened the train windows and threw out books and Bibles to Russian people running alongside it. Today there are Word of Life churches all along that train route!

I remember sharing this testimony at a missions conference in Australia just the other year, and after the session a couple came up to me. Tears were pouring down their faces as they told me in English with a Russian accent: "We were running alongside that train! We were just kids but got hold of a New

Testament, read it, and gave our hearts to Jesus. Today we are pastoring a Russian-speaking church in Melbourne, Australia."

I will never forget that moment. At the same time, I realized that even though this was a story I was lucky enough to hear about, there are so many more that will only be made known in heaven: all the lives who were touched by the money given to missions. All the hearts that found release while you and I were praying for them without their even knowing it. And all the millions of people whose lives were changed because of all the flashlights of the kingdom who accepted their calling and went wherever the Lord told them to go.

So many singles and couples from our church also experienced the flashlight calling to not only visit Russia temporarily on teams but to actually move there—some for life—to serve God's kingdom and help build churches there. Today there are more than three hundred Word of Life churches throughout Russia. None of this would have been possible without the flashlights of the kingdom.

GOD'S FLASHLIGHT IN AFRICA

Throughout history there have been so many amazing examples of what God's flashlights have accomplished as they traveled into the world, shone their lights, and allowed God's power to start moving.

One of them was a young boy named David, born in 1813 in the small Scottish town of Blantyre. Even as a young child he was fascinated by all the undiscovered areas on the world map he studied in school. What about the people who lived in these parts of the world? How unfair that they never got to hear about Jesus.

David and his brother John used to talk about their life goals, and while John had in his mind to get rich and famous,

David only wanted to become a flashlight for God's kingdom. In his twenties, he set out for Africa. He never planned to return home; instead his mind was all focused on giving the rest of his life to fulfill the calling of a missionary and lead as many souls as possible to faith in Christ.

So much can be said about David's efforts. He explored the Zambezi River, discovered Victoria Falls, and constantly sent maps back home to England, providing knowledge that no one in the Western world had ever seen or heard of. Still, his first passion was always to preach the gospel.

Back in the UK he became a celebrity because of his unique exploits. National papers wrote about him constantly and published everything he sent back from Africa. The royal family was eager to meet him, but David himself was blissfully unaware of the commotion he had caused. A journalist named Stanley was sent to Africa to try to track David down, tell him about his celebrity status back in his homeland, and urge him to come home. But David was not interested. He was where God wanted him to be, shining his light, so why should he leave?

David finally finished his race and went to be with the Lord on May 1, 1873. He died as he was kneeling in prayer at his bedside. After removing his heart and burying it close to where he died—because as the natives would say, "His heart was always with us"—a caravan of African men carried his body over one thousand miles for sixty-three days so that it could be sent home by ship to be buried in his homeland. This in itself was a powerful statement of honor and of the change the gospel had brought about, since according to the old native religion of the locals, you were not even allowed to go near a dead body.

Back in England, David Livingstone was buried in Westminster Abbey—the great national shrine where kings, queens, and the true celebrities of British history are put to rest. But contrary to most of the others buried there, whose graves are normally found along the side walls of the cathedral, David is buried right in the middle of the nave, and his grave is among the very first you will see if you pay a visit. His life is a true testament that when you choose the flashlight calling and dare to give up something for God, He will reward you. Whoever loses his life will truly find it.

So what about David's brother John, who wanted to become rich and famous? Well, he did. Then he died. And his tombstone reads: "Here lies John Livingstone, David Livingstone's brother."

Indeed, many who are first will be last, and many who are last will be first (Matt. 19:30).

Thank You, God, for the flashlights of the kingdom!

Chapter 22

THE DARKROOM LIGHT BULB

*T*HE NEXT LIGHT bulb in the kingdom is one I am so thankful for: the darkroom light bulb.

This is quite an unusual lamp. It is covered by a thick layer of dark red plastic material so that when you turn it on, rather than shining bright, it only glows with a warm red light.

You might wonder what the point is of having a light bulb whose light is so dimmed that one can hardly see if it is on or not. But this bulb has a very specific purpose: it is an integral part of developing photos in a darkroom.

The traditional way of developing negatives into photographic pictures is by using instruments such as an enlarger, a focus finder, and trays, and this equipment is used inside a room that is almost completely dark. Why? Because the film of the camera is supersensitive to regular light, and its contents would be instantly destroyed from being exposed to it. However, the red light of the darkroom light bulb is designed to not damage the film and is a vital part of the sensitive developing process—and seeing blank white photo papers suddenly come alive with color, motive, and beauty.

And that is the exact purpose of the darkroom light bulbs in God's kingdom as well. They are designed to shine a delicate, warm light that is part of developing gifts, callings, confidence, strength, self-esteem, boldness, and so much more in the lives of people who did not know they even had that in them. The dark-room light bulb can look at a sheet of photo paper, and while others might say, "It's just blank; there's nothing there but a hopeless case," it sees the potential of change and beauty. It has

179

no greater joy than seeing blank paper humans—maybe torn apart by their former lifestyles, maybe addicts, maybe betrayed to the point where they cannot trust anyone, maybe victims of abuse—and being part of restoring that which was broken, then developing all the beauty God has placed inside them. And when the darkroom light bulbs shine their special light, God will start to work life-changing miracles.

Even though we see Jesus Himself shining the light of every single light bulb mentioned so far, I especially love that the beautiful darkroom light kept shining from His life, warming, touching, and developing the blank paper people of His society, the ones no one else believed in and counted on.

We see Him shining the darkroom light on the woman caught in adultery (John 8:1–11), on Zacchaeus (Luke 19:1–10), on the woman by the well in Samaria (John 4:4–26), on Mary Magdalene (Luke 8:2), and we see that amazing, developing light shine on the twelve young Jewish men that followed Him, turning them from simple fishermen, carpenters, and tax collectors into world changers and history makers.

And how we need an army of darkroom light bulbs in this time and age!

Never before in the history of man has there been a time so full of confusion, lies, torment, depression, identity crises, fear, and lack (or complete loss) of self-esteem. When we pray for revival, the people who will fill our churches—should God answer our prayers—are those battered and bruised by all these tendencies of the world. And if so, we need to make sure the dark lamps of the kingdom are mobilized and ready to shine their special, caring light on the blank sheets and watch them develop into the original colors and contours God intended for their lives.

THE GOD OF GENERATIONS

Another important calling on the darkroom light bulbs of the kingdom is that of shining their developing light on the next generation.

You see, God is and always has been a God of generations. We see that throughout the Bible, maybe clearer than ever in His words to Abraham:

> I will establish my covenant as an everlasting covenant between me and you and your descendants after you for the generations to come, to be your God and the God of your descendants after you.
>
> —GENESIS 17:7

And in how the Lord asks Moses to introduce Him to the Israelites:

> God also said to Moses, "Say to the Israelites, 'The LORD, the God of your fathers—the God of Abraham, the God of Isaac and the God of Jacob—has sent me to you.' This is my name forever, the name you shall call me from generation to generation."
>
> —EXODUS 3:15

He is not just the God of one single man or one single generation but the God of ongoing generations.

God's heart, nature, and ambition is to see His kingdom move through the ages and the generations, not up and down like a roller coaster, but from glory to glory. Still, this will not happen by itself, which is exactly why God keeps reminding His covenant people to do whatever they can to bridge the gap of generations and make sure the kingdom moves swiftly and strongly from one generation to the next.

That you may tell your children and grandchildren
how I dealt harshly with the Egyptians and how I performed my signs among them, and that you may know
that I am the LORD.

—EXODUS 10:2

Only be careful, and watch yourselves closely so that
you do not forget the things your eyes have seen or let
them fade from your heart as long as you live. Teach
them to your children and to their children after them.

—DEUTERONOMY 4:9

We will not hide them from their descendants; we will
tell the next generation the praiseworthy deeds of the
LORD, his power, and the wonders he has done. He
decreed statutes for Jacob and established the law in
Israel, which he commanded our ancestors to teach
their children, so the next generation would know
them, even the children yet to be born, and they in
turn would tell their children.

—PSALM 78:4–6

SPIRITUAL MOTHERS AND FATHERS

This part of the darkroom light bulb calling is one we all share.
For the kingdom to move strongly from one generation to the
next, we need way more than a good children's ministry in
church or a motivated youth pastor. We need to realize that
every single one of us that is not young anymore shares the
responsibility of being a mother or father figure in the church.
I am not just talking about the responsibility for your own natural children but the one that has to do with praying for and
shining the encouraging darkroom light on all the young people

around you, allowing God to turn the parent heart inside you to the children (Mal. 4:6).

This doesn't mean you have to pretend to be young and cool if you're not. Believe me, there is nothing more pathetic than an eighty-year-old with leather pants and a pierced eyebrow. The young of this generation do not need a new friend but a mother or father, a grandmother or grandfather, that will bring stability, faith, encouragement, and prayers into their ever shaking, ever changing reality. They need the soft but steady darkroom light, developing their faith and inspiring them to take new steps in their walk with Jesus. And when they have fallen, to encourage them to rise up and try again.

This theme of building a generational church and seeing the next generation rise up and do exploits for God is one of the strongest themes of my life and ministry. My greatest reward is still to see young people take steps of faith for the glory of the name of Jesus and know that I was blessed enough to play a little part, to add some inspiration, to shine a darkroom light so that God's power could start working in and through that teenager.

Several years ago when we launched the national student ministry New Generation, we saw it spread like wildfire way faster than expected and realized that we needed to expand the manpower rapidly. Hence, as its very first academic year came to a close and hundreds of these Christian school groups had started, we reached out to some of the young people who had started groups but were now about to graduate high school and invited them to come on board as one-year volunteers.

As schools were about to start again after summer, eleven eighteen- and nineteen-year-olds were ready to join New Generation to travel around the nation and visit all its new groups to coach and inspire them. These young mentors came from different cities and different denominations, and most of them didn't know each other beforehand, so we decided to have them live together in the same house throughout the year so they would become close friends fast.

As we prepared for this, my wife, Maria, shared a thought with me: "Why don't we have these young people all move in with our family for a year?" Initially it sounded completely crazy, but the more I thought and prayed about it, the more it dawned on me that this was the Lord. Said and done, a few weeks later we had eleven teenagers move into our family home, and what followed was a joyride of complete and beautiful chaos. The only private space we had left in our house was now our bedroom, into which our two daughters, aged eleven and thirteen, had also moved, and as soon as you opened its door, there were teenagers everywhere!

We cooked together, cleaned together, laughed together, cried together, and shared life together. Every morning and evening we would pray together, rolling out a large map of Sweden on the floor, laying our hands on it and praying for the young generation of each city, town, and village and for every one of the schools in our country to experience revival.

As weeks turned into months, our hearts became so close. Rather than being organizational leaders, Maria and I became spiritual mother and father figures for these young people, constantly mentoring, coaching, correcting, and inspiring. The darkroom light was on day and night, and we started seeing these teenagers develop a maturity way beyond their years. We saw them take responsibility and grow as they did; we saw them try and fail, try again and succeed. We saw discipline and structure evolve as well as a genuine love for the presence of God.

I could go on for hours and tell you about the beauty of this process, but long story short: even though these young people had only signed up to stay with New Generation for a year, most of them stayed behind for three, four, five—even up to eight years. And these eleven became the pillars and foundation of the entire movement.

When people ask me how in the world New Generation could become the fastest-growing youth movement in the secularized nation of Sweden and go on to hold conferences and events in some of the largest arenas in the country, how it could grow to fifteen thousand members in Sweden and twenty-five thousand internationally within years, I always go back to that group of eleven teenagers. And I am reminded of how much color, motive, and beauty God can call forth in young people if only someone is willing to shine that warm, developing light into their lives.

Thank You, God, for the darkroom light bulbs of the kingdom!

Chapter 23

THE CANDLE

*T*HE NEXT REFLECTION of God's great kingdom of light is the candle.

Compared to most of the lights we have talked about so far, the candle stands out in the way its light is not electrical and artificial but emerges from an authentic fire. In a way, this is the OG light, the natural, original version of what a light source is all about.

The candle represents purity, authenticity, legitimacy, and truth, all of which are so needed in this shallow time and age, which is chock-full of clichés and fake filters. The candle shines from a genuine fire that can't be copied or forged, and in doing so it spreads a unique light that not only removes darkness but also adds warmth to cold souls.

Now, whereas all the light bulbs and lamps I have mentioned previously might represent different personalities, every single one of us is called to share the essence and calling of the candle and make sure the life we live is genuine and authentic.

GOLD ALL THE WAY THROUGH

Many years ago my family and I went on holiday to the island of Cyprus. While we were there we visited a crazy water park with slides and rides so fast and wild that social authorities would have closed it down a long time ago if they had known about it.

We had great fun and went on all the hysterical water slides they had, but at the end of the day I went down one so fast that as the slide launched me into the pool below, I broke a finger off the water surface. Even more unfortunate, it was the ring finger of my left hand—the one with my wedding band—and I simply had to cut it off (the ring, not the finger) so it wouldn't damage the finger, which had now begun to swell up.

When I saw the cut edges of the ring, I noticed it was gold all the way through. This in itself was of course no surprise, but it reminded me of something: the definition of real gold, genuine gold, is that it must be gold all the way through, the same material on both the outside and the inside.

That definition is the same for a real, genuine Christian, someone who is made of the same material all the way through. On the outside, what everybody sees, and on the inside—the hidden life only you and God know about.

When Jesus walked this earth, the devil was not His greatest problem. The Bible records just one direct confrontation between him and Jesus straight after the baptism (Matthew 4), then the devil left him.

Jesus didn't have any problems with sinners either. He forgave them time and again, and they repented by the thousands and became His followers. Nowhere in the Gospels do we see Jesus turning anyone away because he or she was too much of a sinner.

The big challenge Jesus faced were the ones called the Pharisees. We can hardly read a single page in the Gospels without the Pharisees and Jesus clashing. So why would the Holy Spirit, who inspired the authors of the New Testament, want so many of these occasions documented? Could it be because He wants to tell us something?

A lot of times we look at the Pharisees as the bad guys. In Jesus movies they are easily recognized by their long black robes and pale gray beards, always pointing their bony fingers at Jesus and shouting. That is actually a pretty convenient perspective as it makes the Pharisees feel far away from us, our world, and reality. And when Jesus confronts them, we assume it has nothing to do with us. Whatever He says to this weird group of people is clearly their problem and not ours.

But let's try to honestly find out what the real problem was with the Pharisees and what caused Jesus to be so harsh with them. Look carefully at this passage:

> Woe to you, teachers of the law and Pharisees, you hypocrites! You clean the outside of the cup and dish, but inside they are full of greed and self-indulgence. Blind Pharisee! First clean the inside of the cup and dish, and then the outside also will be clean. Woe to you, teachers of the law and Pharisees, you hypocrites! You are like whitewashed tombs, which look beautiful on the outside but on the inside are full of the bones of the dead and everything unclean. In the same way, on the outside you appear to people as righteous but on the inside you are full of hypocrisy and wickedness.
>
> —MATTHEW 23:25–28

Wow. I would not want to be on the receiving end of Jesus' words here. But let's have a close look and ask ourselves: What is it that makes Jesus so upset? Do you see what He constantly comes back to? Again and again, He is referring to the fact that the outside and the inside of the Pharisees had become two totally different things. They were working to polish what could be seen but could not care less about the inside. In other words, they had stopped being genuine, stopped being real, stopped being the same all the way through.

It was this very thing—not the black robes, gray beards, or bony fingers—that was their problem in the eyes of Christ. Though their movement had started as a genuine revival during the Maccabees' time in between the Old and New Testaments, eventually they ended up opposing the God they so fervently claimed to serve. As a result they did not even recognize His own Son when He was standing right in front of them.

So why then does God detest a double life, and why does He love that which is genuine? The answer is quite simple: because He Himself is genuine. He is the same all the way through. He is light, and in Him there is no darkness at all.

ATTRACTED TO THE GENUINE

God is not the only one who looks for what is genuine and real. The whole world is attracted by it, because deep down we are all created to live genuine, real, and honest lives—ones that are the same all the way through.

The longing to be real can even take people so far as to follow insane ideologies, just to feel that they get to be radical and genuine. Why did so many youths follow destructive leaders such as Hitler, Stalin, Lenin, and many others? Because they were real, passionate, and genuine about the immoral and ungodly things they believed in, and young people were attracted by it.

On the other hand, people who claim to have a faith and conviction but are really just keeping up nice appearances have a very low status in this world. This is what had happened to the Pharisees, and it resulted in a whole society associating God and His kingdom with empty words, laws, and regulations without life and power.

Jesus reacted strongly against this, and the ones He sent out instead to represent His kingdom and preach His gospel were simple, non-professional, and very imperfect people. But they were genuine: Genuine in their passion for Him. Genuine in having seen and heard something they could not keep quiet about (Acts 4:20). Genuine in the way that, when they failed and fell, they did not try to excuse and cover up their mistakes but repented and ran back to Jesus. They were genuine candles.

Our world is longing to see genuine Christians, real candles in their own generation. Praise God for professional pastors, evangelists, and preachers, but no one could be a stronger testimony for Jesus than someone who is part of the everyday life and reality of your friends, neighbors, fellow students, work colleagues, and family members. It is in your lifestyle and values that they will look for what is genuine. Your lifestyle may be the only Bible they will ever read.

The world does not require you to answer all questions, succeed in everything you do, or seem invulnerable, but it does need to see that you are real in your relationship with God.

This is why it is so important that you and I look through our lives regularly, noting what is genuine and what is just a mask, then dare to hand those masks to Jesus and ask Him for the power to transform that part of our life (or lifestyle) into something that is real, genuine, and the same all the way through so that our candle can light up the way to the house of the Father.

Thank You, God, for the candles of the kingdom!

Chapter 24

THE WEIRD LIGHT BULB

*W*E ARE COMING to the close of this list of light bulbs and lamps in the kingdom of God, all there to display His diversity and to light up the world. But let me tell you: there are so many more! The kingdom of God contains such a beautiful range of lights, lamps, personalities, gifts—all perfectly designed by the Creator and made for "such a time as this" (Est. 4:14). I will paraphrase John the Evangelist in saying that if we mentioned them all, "even the whole world would not have room for the books that would be written" (John 21:25). Still, I pray you have been inspired, encouraged, broadened in your perspective, and maybe even discovered yourself in one or more of the light bulbs mentioned.

However, I cannot end this short list of mine without another one of my favorites within the family of God's light bulbs: the weird one.

As I share this illustrated message around the world and present this bright green bulb with black silicone spikes as the last one in the lineup, I always see loving smiles on the faces of the attendees, as they understand the character and personality I am trying to portray. We all know a weird light bulb, and most of us have been one at some phase of our life—and to some extent most of us still are.

The weird light bulb is a special addition to the family of lights. These individuals often have an underlying feeling—sometimes from their surroundings, sometimes from themselves—that they don't fit in because they're not really like those around them. And the more streamlined the world becomes, the more everyone is pressured to be identical and not stand out, the more the weird light bulb does just that. It stands out.

When others hang out at the mall, go out to eat in a group, or see the latest blockbuster movie together, the weird light bulb might rather stay at home watching Belgian black-and-white films from the 1940s, admire its collection of Star Wars figurines, or play *Zelda* on a Game Boy Advance from 2001.

The weird light bulb does not feel the need to follow trends, be like everyone else, or try hard to fit in. It celebrates originality and being true to who you are. It might well see other light bulbs as shallow and mere copies of one another, while those other ones are likely to leave the weird light bulb out because it's so different and not like them.

Because the weird light bulb is different, it is sometimes tempted to feel there is no place for it in the kingdom—that God only uses other lamps and light bulbs but not green ones with black silicone spikes.

But let me tell you, He does!

Throughout the entire Bible, God almost exclusively used unexpected people, the ones this world—and sometimes even God's people—ruled out as hopeless, weird, and unqualified. Abram was the most illogical choice to be a father of nations. David was the weirdest combatant to set against Goliath. Mary was completely unqualified to have a child. Gideon was a coward in all but God's eyes. Not to mention that completely weird group of twelve guys who were given the task to go out into the world and change it through the power of the gospel.

The weird light bulbs that we sometimes place, or who place themselves, on the outskirts of our churches are actually right at the center of biblical history and its story of salvation.

So let me tell you who sometimes feel different and that you are not fit for church, you who are sometimes isolated (and who sometimes isolate yourself from others because you are not exactly like them), and you who might have given up hope of being used by God:

You can shine!

You have been perfectly designed by God for the time and place you are in. You have been given a unique light to shine, and when you do, God's power will start to move. There is someone out there waiting to see that light of Jesus through you, someone no other light bulb or lamp will be able to reach.

So don't let the devil or anyone else tell you differently. You are called, chosen, equipped, and fit for the kingdom, and the only one who can stop you from fulfilling that calling and reaching that goal of your destiny is you. Don't isolate yourself, and don't allow yourself to be isolated. Be faithful in your church, find friends, fuel your heart with God's Word and presence, and take the initiatives that come your way. If you do, you will be surprised at how much God will be able to accomplish through that light shining through you!

ANNICA'S RED PAPER HEARTS

Some years ago I met a teenage girl called Annica. She was from another part of Sweden but came to attend one of our youth conferences, and I immediately noticed her during worship, as she was using sign language to worship God. Later she came up to me, we talked, and I learned that she was completely deaf in one ear and had only about 20 percent hearing capacity in the other. Annica was also completely blind in one eye and had about 20 percent vision in the other. Medically speaking, she was almost deaf and almost blind. But most importantly, she loved Jesus with all her heart.

Annica had a beautiful encounter with Jesus during the conference. She rededicated her heart to follow Him closer and to shine His light like never before. And with this new commitment she went back to her hometown and her school for students with seeing and hearing disabilities. Sure, a voice inside her tried to tell her that she was not cut out to serve God—what could she ever accomplish for His kingdom, barely being able to see or hear? But for the first time in her life Annica did not listen. She refused to reduce herself to a victim of life when Jesus called her the light of the world!

Annica prayed for ideas and opportunities to share Jesus and shine for God by taking an initiative in her school. Quite soon she chose Valentine's Day as an excuse to celebrate the love of God. After all, what day could be better to talk about the greatest love of all?

This was November, so she had about three months to prepare her project. Step number one was to cut out two-hundred-plus red paper hearts, one for each student in her school. Her second move was to get a list of the names of all the students at her school from the office and personalize each paper heart by writing one student name on each one. But the third step was what brought tears to my eyes when I heard her story: Annica took each heart, read the name on it, and asked God what He wanted to say to this specific girl or boy. What did that person need to hear from God more than anything? What would make the strongest impact on this heart and communicate the love of Jesus more than anything at this very moment?

Even though Annica herself only knew a fraction of the students personally, she realized that the Holy Spirit knew them all inside out. So she asked Him and then just remained in God's presence until she received a thought and a few words that she dared to believe to be from God Himself for this specific student. She wrote the message down on the paper heart, then picked up the next one, asked God for His guidance on what to write, and again waited until she picked up another impulse or thought, trusting it was the still small voice of the Holy Spirit.

During the course of the next three months, Annica prayed for every single one of the teenagers that attended her school.

When Valentine's Day finally arrived, Annica brought her personalized paper hearts to school and throughout the day handed them out to every single student. When she told me this story herself some months later, she said, "You know, pastor, it's so great that all the students in my school communicate through sign language. This enabled me to go around all day and see what everyone was talking about!"

And all over the school, throughout the whole day, she saw young people in groups talking to one another, saying things like, "How in the world could this girl know what I'm going through?" "I don't believe it! Those words she wrote felt like they were just for me!" "Who could have told her exactly what I needed to hear?"

It turned out that once again God had chosen the weak things of this world to shame the strong (1 Cor. 1:27). He had used what many would consider a weird light bulb, someone different and outside the norm—a fourteen-year-old girl who could hardly see or hear—to plant the seed of the gospel in over two hundred hearts that neither you nor I would probably ever reach.

And let me tell you, friend: if Annica could shine for Jesus, so can you!

Thank You, God, for all the weird light bulbs of the kingdom!

Chapter 25

NOW GO LIGHT UP YOUR WORLD!

*J*OHANNA SMILED AS she walked down the pedestrian street that forms the center of her town. The air felt fresh, and so did her sixteen-year-old heart.

She and two friends had just attended a youth conference and felt God challenge them to start letting their light shine like never before and dare to believe that His power and presence would be released as they did. When they got back home, the girl trio decided to meet once a week to pray for revival, and Johanna was now on her way to their weekly prayer meeting.

She felt the breeze in her long brown hair and how her heart was thrumming with anticipation. Oh man, life was exciting! Not always easy, to be sure—Johanna had already had a few ups and downs—but that inner motivation that had come from getting her heart right with God at the conference, making some new life decisions, and now doing her very best to back them up...it felt good, inspiring.

Prayers bubbled up inside her as she made her way through the shopping crowds in the street. The excitement made her heart almost burst as she stopped, closed her eyes, and whispered, "God, use me now!"

Then she opened her eyes slowly and looked around, hoping God would answer her prayer and somehow use her at that very moment, though she had no idea how or what she expected to happen.

But immediately she saw something unusual—a girl her age, coming toward her in the crowd. Johanna had never seen her before, but the girl stood out. She was crying. And talking to someone on her phone. As I've said many times, showing emotion in public really makes you stand out in Sweden. People mind their own business and definitely avoid outbursts of emotion.

Johanna was now trying to process what she saw. For some reason this girl was crying and coming her way, about to pass by her in just seconds. Everything Swedish inside of Johanna panicked and cried out, "Don't intervene! Don't get involved! Look the other way!" But her newly refreshed and renewed heart whispered, "It's time to shine your light."

So Johanna did the only thing she could think of. Looking at the girl, she threw both her arms out wide like an invitation to a massive hug. Part of her felt awkward, scared, and embarrassed, but her insides smiled and so did her face. The crying girl saw her, stopped for half a second, and then walked right into the embrace of Johanna's open arms.

Two complete strangers were now standing there hugging and holding one another. One was sobbing; the other one wondered what in the world she would do now. What was the next step after hugging a complete stranger on a pedestrian street in Sweden?

Johanna prayed silently, seeking the Lord's advice, then whispered into the ear of the crying girl: "Would you like to come along to meet my friends?" The girl was crying so hard she could not even speak, but Johanna felt her head nodding against her shoulder, and the two girls started slowly walking together.

At her friend's house, Johanna quickly updated the other two on what had happened and said this could not possibly be a coincidence. The girl had appeared the second Johanna asked to be used by God, so there had to be a special meaning to it.

The three girls held the fourth one and prayed for her, told her whatever was wrong Jesus could help her through, and shared the gospel with her. The girl did not say much about herself or the reason she was crying. Instead she listened carefully until about a half hour later she said she had to leave. She and Johanna exchanged email addresses and promised to stay in touch.

One week later Johanna received a long email from the girl, sharing for the first time the full story of what had actually happened that day. How she was really on her way home to lock herself in her room and commit suicide.

Though she was only sixteen years old, she had come to a place where life did not make sense anymore and just hurt too much for her to move on and keep trying. Parents, friends, and boyfriends had all failed her to the point where she felt she could not take anymore. She might as well end it.

Piece by piece a plan had unfolded in her mind about how she would pick a certain date as her last day ever. That morning inside her room she would prepare everything needed to end her own life, then go to school as on any other day. She would stay in the shadows the way she always did, anonymous and quiet, and nobody but her would have a clue that these were her last few hours on earth. When the school day was over, she would walk her regular route back home through the town center, and right before she came to the door of her house she would make a final phone call to her aunt, the only one who had ever shown her love and care. She would tell her thank you and goodbye, but she had made careful calculations that even if her aunt tried to come stop her, or call someone else to do so, it would already be too late. She would already be gone forever.

When Johanna had opened her eyes on that pedestrian street, this girl had been in the middle of that final call to her aunt, and with only minutes left to live she was crying as she told her goodbye forever.

"But then," the girl wrote in the email, "I looked up. And I saw you."

She did not see Jesus. Nor Billy Graham. Nor a full-time pastor or an evangelist with a global ministry.

She saw a regular girl, part of her own time and generation, who had made herself available to be a light in the hands of God and to shine this light brightly by giving God an initiative He could bless and use. This unknown girl had made herself available to throw her arms out wide, proclaiming "Let there be light!" into a darkness she was not even aware of.

"And I didn't know why, Johanna, but I walked straight into those open arms of yours," the girl wrote. "And then you hugged me and held me. And when you did, I felt the first tiny glimpse of hope that I had experienced in years. That maybe I belong. Maybe there is love and purpose after all."

She kept writing about how she had realized this could not be a coincidence, how this Jesus she was told about must love her so much He placed Johanna right in front of her with arms wide open, as if love had blocked the way to her planned suicide. She ended the email by writing: "I think I need to get to know this Jesus."

Johanna got to lead her to faith in Christ, and the life of the girl was literally saved twice. Once physically, once eternally.

WITH ARMS STRETCHED WIDE

I will never forget when Johanna told me this story sometime later, how it blew me away and brought tears to my eyes. I looked at her and said, "Johanna, when you were standing there on that pedestrian street with your arms out, you represented someone. One who stretched His arms out wide on a cross two thousand years ago and who still has His arms wide open to receive whoever will come."

And that, my friend, is what this whole book has been about.

Not about seven principles to grow a fortune. Not about a master class in how to get God to fulfill all your dreams and desires. But about the calling that I know resonates deep inside your heart right now:

To step up, step out, and be the light of the world that Jesus calls you to be.

To shine your unique light through the gifts and personality God has given you, whatever light bulb or lamp He has called you to be.

To give Him an initiative in your world that He can bless and magnify, that initial step of faith that turns the light on and allows God's power to move.

To let your light shine bright like a city on a hill, and in doing so block the way of darkness and despair and throw open wide the arms of Jesus' love toward your world.

Let us shine for His glory!

Let us shine for His kingdom!

Let us shine until that final, glorious morning when the night is over once and for all and death and darkness are finally swallowed into the marvelous light of our God.

> There will be no more night. They will not need the light of a lamp or the light of the sun, for the Lord God will give them light. And they will reign for ever and ever.

> —REVELATION 22:5

NOTES

1. "Leaflets of the White Rose," White Rose Foundation, accessed July 12, 2024, https://www.weisse-rose-stiftung.de/white-rose-resistance-group/leaflets-of-the-white-rose/.
2. "Sophie Scholl Quotes," Goodreads, accessed July 12, 2024, https://www.goodreads.com/author/quotes/801549. Sophie_Scholl.
3. Sara Barratt, "75 Years Ago Today: The Incredible Story of Hans and Sophie Scholl," TGC, February 22, 2018, https://www.thegospelcoalition.org/article/75-years-ago-hans-sophie-scholl/.
4. "Sophie Scholl Quotes," Goodreads.

ABOUT THE AUTHOR

*J*OAKIM LUNDQVIST IS pastor and international ambassador of Word of Life Church in Uppsala, Sweden. Even in this extremely secularized nation, the church has built an international network of over nine hundred churches worldwide.

Word of Life puts its main focus on building the kingdom of God and shining His light where it's needed the most, in nations such as Afghanistan, Iraq, China, India, Iran, and Ukraine.

An inspiring speaker, Joakim has visited over fifty nations throughout the world. His thirty years of experience in youth ministry shine through in his creative messages, which have the ability to relate to every generation. He is also the author of four books that have been translated into several languages.

Joakim and his wife, Maria, have been married for more than thirty-five years. They have two grown-up daughters, Evelina and Julia, and two grandsons, Zion and Samson.